quick
SLOW
COOKING

Kim Laidlaw

Photographs by Eva Kolenko

weldon**owen**

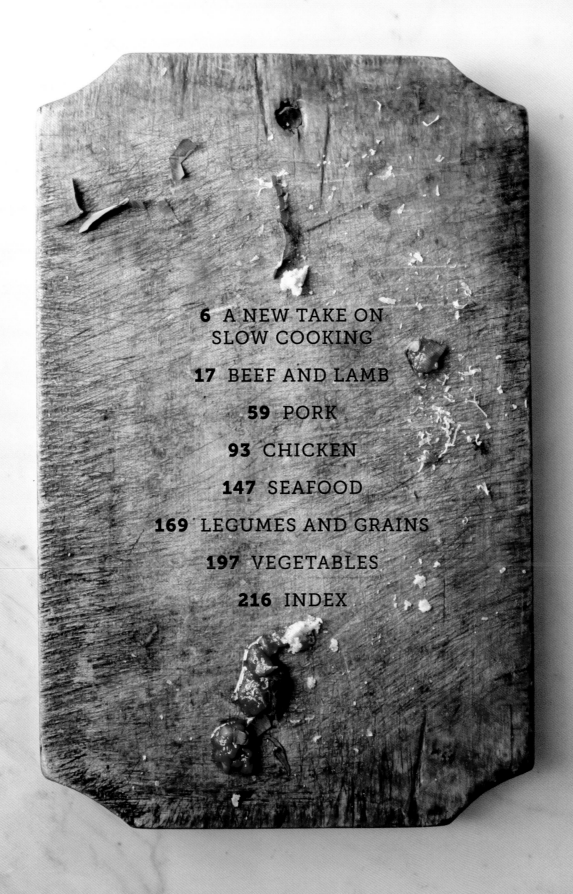

a new take on slow cooking

A slow-cooker book that claims to help you put together a meal quickly sounds like a contradiction. And yes, it's true that start-to-finish times for dishes prepared in a slow cooker are usually pretty long. But the tool itself is a true time-saver for busy cooks. Once the ingredients are in the cooker, they typically require little or no attention until you're nearly ready to sit down and eat.

A slow cooker promises easy preparation and delicious results, a combination that is rarely possible with most cooking methods. When left to cook slowly in seasoned liquids, tough cuts of beef, pork, or lamb become meltingly tender. Chicken takes on deep flavor from the seasonings it simmers in, and fish and shellfish maintain their delicacy in the moist heat. Beans cook like they were meant to, holding their shape yet becoming velvety and full flavored, and the sturdiest vegetables soften in texture and intensify in flavor.

In this new take on slow cooking, you'll find more than 120 recipes developed with the hectic schedule of a home cook in mind. The recipes boast streamlined ingredient lists, a minimum of steps, and are either a one-pot dish or a main course that can be turned into a meal with a purchased or easily assembled side dish. Some of the steps, such as marinating meat or cutting up vegetables, can be done the night before to save time on the day you cook. Browning, which is a great flavor-producing step, is optional whenever possible, so that harried cooks can choose just to assemble the dish, turn on the cooker, and go about their day. Tips and tricks for the busy cook—such as how to choose the best slow cooker, how to plan meals ahead of time, and how to round out the menu of a slow-cooked dinner—will not only save you precious time but also ensure that you can put a satisfying, home-cooked meal on the table.

dinner is just a few steps away

I developed these recipes with the busy cook in mind. Each one consists of six steps or fewer, but many have just two or three steps. Following is a key to the recipe steps and the part that each one plays in my philosophy of quick slow cooking.

PREP This step applies to tasks that are done before an ingredient hits the heat, such as seasoning meat with salt and pepper, dusting it with seasoned flour, or marinating it. It might also include stirring together a handful of ingredients for a sauce or other mixture. Sometimes the prep can be done the night before cooking, which saves you time the next day.

BUILD FLAVOR Browning helps build an extra layer of flavor in a recipe. In some recipes it is optional, but if you have a few extra minutes or if you plan to serve the dish to company, it is worth the time. In other recipes, browning is essential to the success of the dish. Be sure to follow the cues in the recipes.

QUICK COOK Sometimes, a brief initial cooking of aromatic ingredients or vegetables helps to kick-start the slow-cooking process. If you can do this step in the slow-cooker insert rather than in a frying pan, you won't have an extra pan to wash.

SLOW COOK This is the heart of the recipe, the point at which you add the main ingredient, cover the slow cooker, press start, and walk away until the dish is done or nearly done.

ASSEMBLE Some recipes call for one or two last-minute tasks, such as defatting and then simmering the braising liquid to reduce it, slicing a roast, or stirring together ingredients for an accompanying sauce.

SERVE This step offers tips for getting the dish from the cooker to the table in style. It typically includes ideas for serving vessels and an easy finishing touch, such as a sprinkle of chopped herbs, a squeeze of fresh citrus juice, or a drizzle of olive oil.

CHOOSING INGREDIENTS

In keeping with the quick-cooking theme, the recipes in this book have a relatively short list of fresh ingredients, so choose those ingredients with care. I'm of the feeling that the better the quality of the ingredients that you choose, the better your end result. For fresh vegetables, particularly root vegetables, I find that choosing in-season and organic results in fuller flavor and better texture. When it comes to meat, poultry, and seafood, make every effort to choose from sustainable sources—you really can taste the difference, plus it's a healthier option for the environment. Also, when selecting large cuts of meat such as pork shoulder or beef brisket, choose cuts that are well-marbled: you need the fat to keep the meat moist while braising. I prefer bone-in chicken thighs over breasts when using the slow-cooker; the meat stays moist and flavorful and won't dry out. Be sure to remove the skin unless you are browning the meat.

about slow cookers

The recipes in this book are designed for a 6- to 7-quart (6- to 7-liter) slow cooker with a removable cast-aluminum insert and dual temperature setting. These two features allow you to sauté vegetables and other aromatics or brown meats and poultry on the stove top to build flavor and then return the insert to the cooker for long cooking on either the low-heat setting (about 170°F/77°C) or the high-heat setting (about 280°F/138°C). If you have a smaller slow cooker, you can easily halve many of the recipes (unless you're cooking a large roast) without changing the cooking time. I prefer to cook most recipes on the low-heat setting, which helps deliver fuller flavors and render tough cuts of meat meltingly tender.

When making any recipe, be sure to follow the directions for temperature setting and for timing, as they are the keys to safe and successful slow cooking. Some recipes offer both a low-heat option and a high-heat option to make it easier to fit them into your schedule. Today's slow cookers tend to cook at higher temperatures than the slow cookers manufactured in previous years. Bear this in mind if you are preparing the recipes in this book using an older model—you may need to add to the overall cooking time, or select the high-heat setting and decrease the cooking time slightly. It is also important to read carefully through the instruction book that came with your slow cooker. It will detail the product's features, information that will help you get the most out of the appliance.

The dual-temperature feature is a boon for the busy cook, making it easier to tailor slow cooking to any schedule: the high-heat setting completes cooking in roughly half the time of the low-heat setting. Recipes that specify low heat are typically ideal for when you want to turn on the cooker early in the day, before you leave the house, so that they are ready by dinnertime. High-heat recipes are especially practical for weekends, when you may want to start the cooker in the afternoon for dinnertime. Many models also have a warm setting that holds food at the ideal serving temperature, automatically switching to it when cooking is done.

If your slow cooker does not have a removable insert, or if the removable insert is not safe for stove-top use, you can still successfully prepare the recipes in this book using a good-sized frying pan for the Build Flavor and Quick Cook steps. For the best results, use a large-diameter, heavy pan made from a nonreactive material that conducts heat well, such as stainless steel, anodized aluminum, or enamel-coated cast iron.

CARING FOR YOUR SLOW COOKER

The glazed stoneware insert, or cooking crock, of a slow cooker is made to stand up well under prolonged low-heat cooking conditions. But the material from which it is made is sensitive to extreme temperatures or to sudden changes of temperature, which can cause it to crack or break. To avoid mishaps, follow the instructions from the manufacturer and do not put the insert over the direct heat of a stove top unless it is specifically designed for stove-top cooking. Also, never use the insert in a conventional oven or put it into the freezer. When cleaning the insert, handle it with care to avoid chipping or breakage and do not put cold water into it if it is still hot from cooking. Wash the insert with soap and water and a sponge, avoiding abrasives that could scratch the surface.

developing flavor

Efficiency and ease were key goals in the creation of these recipes, but they were never achieved at the expense of great flavor. Each recipe step has been carefully considered to ensure that you are putting a delectable meal on the table with little extra effort. Here are six flavor-developing steps that are commonly used throughout the book.

SEASONING Seasoning is critical to making any dish taste good. Many recipes start by sprinkling the main ingredient with salt and pepper. Others employ a bold spice rub or marinade and an overnight stint in the refrigerator so the flavorful mixture permeates the food. You will also find several robust prepared ingredients—anchovy paste, kimchi, chipotle chiles in adobo sauce, hoisin sauce, and Sriracha, to name only a handful—used to add complexity without adding extra preparation steps. Because slow-cooked recipes are heated for a long time, which tends to dull flavors, you may find that you are adding more spices, herbs, and other aromatics than you would with conventional cooking techniques. That being said, to prevent over-seasoning, it's always a good idea to go easy on the salt at the beginning of cooking, then season a dish to taste just before serving.

BROWNING Browning is an optional step in most of the recipes, and many busy cooks will omit it in favor of getting the ingredients into the slow cooker fast so that they can carry on with their day. But when you have the time, browning is a smart thing to do. It helps develop a richer, more complex, deeper flavor and a more appealing appearance, qualities that enhance the finished recipe.

DEGLAZING When you cook aromatics or brown meats or poultry in the slow-cooker insert, juices and drippings are released, creating delicious browned bits that stick to the hot surface. Often a flavorful liquid, such as broth, wine, or beer, is added to help loosen these bits, which are then stirred up and dissolved in the cooking liquid. This develops the richness of the sauce. Take care not to add too much liquid, as the natural juices from the meat, poultry, and vegetables will add to the volume of the cooking liquid.

SIMMERING A gentle simmer in the controlled heat of a slow cooker is the heart of the cooking process. During this largely unattended time, foods gain a silky texture, their flavors concentrate, and they mingle with the herbs and spices, cooking liquid, aromatics, and other ingredients to create a full-flavored dish. Also, many of the meat and poultry cuts used in slow cooking contain rich veins of fat, collagen, and connective tissue. Slow cooking renders these cuts fork-tender and brings out their natural flavors.

REDUCING Once a dish is ready, occasionally a recipe calls for vigorously simmering the cooking liquid to reduce its volume. This process concentrates flavors and thickens the resulting sauce. If you find that the finished braising juices are too thin to use as a sauce, use a slotted spoon to transfer the solid ingredients to a platter, strain the cooking liquid through a fine-mesh sieve into a saucepan, then skim the fat from the top with a large metal spoon. Simmer the liquid over medium heat until it becomes slightly syrupy, or to your desired consistency.

FINISHING Many slow-cooked recipes gain even more character from adding an ingredient or two—citrus juice, chopped fresh herbs, cream, or coconut milk—toward the end of cooking. Although this requires a tiny bit more effort than the fix-it-and-forget-it approach some busy cooks favor, it does offer a contrasting texture or complementary flavor that helps bring everything together. Garnishing a dish with a scattering of fresh herbs, particularly any that were used in the main dish, a dollop of sour cream, or a sprinkle of shredded cheese, is a quick and easy way to add flavor and beauty to your finished dish as well.

STOCKING THE FREEZER, REFRIGERATOR, AND PANTRY

The secret to quick cooking is being prepared. Keeping your pantry, refrigerator, and freezer well stocked and organized means you will save time when you are ready to cook. Take inventory of what is in your kitchen now, and then tailor how you stock your kitchen to your tastes by choosing items that are used in your favorite dishes. Once your larder is stocked, you'll be able to make your well-loved recipes by purchasing a few fresh ingredients.

rounding out a slow-cooked meal

Once you've decided on the centerpiece of your meal, you can figure out a complementary side dish (or dishes) and how much time you have to prepare it. The great thing about many slow-cooked dishes is that you can gauge exactly when they will be ready to serve and time your accompaniments accordingly.

BREADS Hunks of fresh, crusty bread are great for dunking into saucy dishes. Slice the same bread, pan grill it (or toast it under the broiler), and rub it with a clove of garlic to serve alongside tomato-based dishes or lighter fare. Wedges of sweet corn bread are great with many soups and stews, particularly chili. Warm naan suits Indian-style curries and stews, and corn or flour tortillas, warmed briefly on the stove top or in the oven, are ideal for Latin-style dishes.

COUSCOUS Precooked dried couscous, sometimes called instant or quick-cooking couscous, is available packaged or in bulk. It requires only rehydrating in boiling water before serving. Offer it plain or stir in raisins, currants, toasted chopped nuts, or fresh herbs, depending on the flavors of the main dish.

FRESH VEGETABLES Some slow-cooker dishes include fresh vegetables; others are large cuts of braised meat that will benefit from a side dish of steamed, sautéed, or roasted vegetables. If you have time, roast asparagus, broccoli, Brussels sprouts, cauliflower, or winter squash. If you need something more quickly, steam or stir-fry green vegetables, such as peas, green beans, broccoli, or sugar snap peas, or sauté or braise hearty greens like chard or kale.

PASTA AND NOODLES Dried pasta and egg noodles are a natural match for many slow-cooked dishes. Save time by purchasing fresh noodles, such as fettuccine, which cook in just a few minutes. Some dried rice noodles require only a short time in a bowl of hot water to soften before serving.

POLENTA Polenta forms a tempting, creamy base for a variety of dishes. Cooked the traditional way, in simmering water, polenta takes about a half hour of hands-on time, but since the main dish is simmering in the slow cooker, you will have time to tend it. Instant polenta is another option, and because the grains have been parboiled, it takes much less time to prepare. You can also find tubes of cooked polenta in well-stocked supermarkets. They can be sliced, drizzled with olive oil, and baked, pan-fried, or grilled.

POTATOES AND SWEET POTATOES Mashed russet or Yukon gold potatoes are ideal for soaking up the fragrant juices of slow-cooked meats and poultry. Mashed sweet potatoes are wonderful paired with pork and poultry dishes. A baked potato is a sturdy base for vegetarian, poultry, or meat-based chili, and roasted small whole potatoes or sweet potato wedges are good alongside slow-cooked roasts.

PREPARED SIDE DISHES Save time and effort by picking up prepared foods from your local specialty food market or deli to serve as side dishes. Potato salad, coleslaw, baked beans, three-bean salad, and grain and vegetable salads are all wonderful ways to round out a slow-cooked meal.

RICE Basmati, jasmine, or other long-grain rice is an excellent accompaniment to many slow-cooked dishes, especially those with Latin and Asian flavors.

SALAD A big green salad complements a wide range of dishes and is a great way to add nutrients to a meal. Consider, too, vegetable- and fruit-based salads, such as sliced tomatoes and cucumbers with olives, thinly sliced fennel and red onion with orange segments, or avocado, papaya, and jicama with pecans.

OTHER IDEAS Fried, poached, or soft-boiled eggs add heft and protein to bean, grain, or vegetable dishes. Seasoned and simmered black beans pair well with dishes with Latin or Caribbean flavors.

Beef
AND
Lamb

Smoky Joes

Who doesn't love a good homemade Sloppy Joe? This version takes the classic up a notch with the addition of smoky chipotle chiles in adobo sauce. If you prefer a milder dish, use only 1 chipotle chile and remove the seeds before mincing. For traditional Sloppy Joes, omit the chipotles chiles and adobo sauce and increase the chili powder to 2 tablespoons. I like to top my Smoky Joe with a slice of Monterey jack cheese.

ingredients

1 tablespoon olive oil

1½ yellow onions, finely chopped

2 ribs celery, finely chopped

1 small red bell pepper, seeded and finely chopped

1 small green bell pepper, seeded and finely chopped

Kosher salt and freshly ground pepper

3 lb (1.5 kg) lean ground beef

2 cups (16 fl oz/500 ml) tomato sauce

1 cup (8 oz/250 g) tomato ketchup

2 chipotle chiles in adobo sauce, minced, plus 1 tablespoon adobo sauce

2 tablespoons Worcestershire sauce

2 tablespoons whole-grain mustard

1 tablespoon cider vinegar

2 tablespoons golden brown sugar

4 teaspoons chili powder

10–12 burger buns, split

makes 10—12 servings

step by step

QUICK COOK Put the slow-cooker insert on the stove top over medium-high heat, then add the oil and warm until hot. Add the onions, celery, red and green bell peppers, and a big pinch of salt and cook, stirring, until the vegetables have softened, about 5 minutes. Using a slotted spoon, transfer the vegetables to a bowl and set aside.

Add the beef to the oil remaining in the insert and cook, stirring and breaking it up with a wooden spoon, until it is no longer pink, 8—10 minutes. Remove from the heat and stir in the reserved vegetables.

SLOW COOK Transfer the insert to the slow cooker and add the tomato sauce, ketchup, chipotle chiles and adobo sauce, Worcestershire sauce, mustard, vinegar, sugar, chili powder, 2 teaspoons salt, and ¼ cup (2 fl oz/60 ml) water. Stir to mix well. Cover and cook on the low-heat setting for 6 hours.

ASSEMBLE When the beef mixture is ready, toast the buns.

SERVE Spoon some of the beef mixture onto the bottom half of each toasted bun. Cover with the bun tops and serve right away.

Chili-Rubbed Brisket Tacos

Tucked into warm tortillas, this tender brisket does not need much embellishment. Instead of folded into tacos, you could top the meat with barbecue sauce in burger buns or arrange it on top of a Mexican-inspired salad. This recipe yields enough to feed a crowd and also freezes well. Be sure to choose a well-marbled brisket, as the fat will keep the meat tender and moist.

ingredients

2 tablespoons chili powder

1 tablespoon coarsely ground pepper

1 tablespoon sugar

1 tablespoon onion powder

2 teaspoons dry mustard

Kosher salt

1 center-cut beef brisket, about 6 lb (3 kg), fat layer trimmed to ½ inch (12 mm) thick

1 yellow onion, finely chopped

1 bottle (12 fl oz/375 ml) lager-style beer

Corn or flour tortillas, about 6 inches (15 cm) in diameter, warmed

Pickled red onions, jalapeño slices, thinly sliced radishes, fresh cilantro leaves, tomatillo salsa, sour cream, or other favorite taco toppings for serving

makes 8–10 servings

step by step

PREP In a small bowl, stir together the chili powder, pepper, sugar, onion powder, dry mustard, and 1 tablespoon salt until well combined. Rub the brisket all over with the spice mixture. Cut the brisket in half crosswise, then wrap both halves in aluminum foil or place in an airtight container and refrigerate overnight or up to 24 hours.

SLOW COOK Transfer the brisket halves to a slow cooker, placing them in as even a layer as possible. Sprinkle the onion over the top and pour the beer into the cooker along the edge of the insert. Cover and cook on the low-heat setting for 8—10 hours. The brisket should be fork-tender.

ASSEMBLE Transfer the brisket to a platter. Using 2 forks, shred the brisket into bite-size pieces, discarding any large pieces of fat. Using a large spoon, spoon off and discard as much fat as possible from the surface of the cooking liquid. Moisten the brisket with some of the warm cooking liquid. Assemble the taco toppings.

SERVE Set the platter of brisket on the table. Accompany with tortillas and the toppings for diners to make their own tacos.

Picadillo

Picadillo is a much-loved dish found in many Latin countries, from Cuba to Mexico, as well as my home state of Texas. It is often served over rice, but I like it tucked into warm soft flour tortillas or spooned onto crisp fried corn tostada shells and topped with shredded lettuce, avocado slices, and a big squeeze of lime.

ingredients

1 tablespoon olive oil

1 large yellow onion, finely chopped

1 large poblano chile, seeded and finely chopped

Kosher salt

3 lb (1.5 kg) lean ground beef

1 lb (500 g) Yukon gold potatoes (about 3), peeled and cut into ½-inch (12-mm) cubes

1 can (15 oz/470 g) crushed tomatoes with juice

1 jalapeño chile, seeded and minced

2 cloves garlic, minced

1 tablespoon cumin

¼ cup (1½ oz/45 g) dried currants

½ cup (2½ oz/75 g) pitted and sliced green olives

¼ cup (⅓ oz/10 g) chopped fresh cilantro

2 tablespoons distilled white vinegar

makes 6 servings

step by step

QUICK COOK Put the slow-cooker insert over medium-high heat, then add the oil and warm until hot. Add the onion, poblano chile, and a large pinch of salt and cook, stirring occasionally, until the onion starts to brown, about 6 minutes. Add the beef and cook, stirring and breaking up the meat with a wooden spoon, until browned, about 5 minutes.

SLOW COOK Transfer the insert to the slow cooker, add the potatoes, tomatoes, jalapeño chile, garlic, cumin, and 2 teaspoons salt, and stir to mix well. Cover and cook on the low-heat setting for 5½ hours.

Uncover the slow cooker, add the currants, olives, cilantro, and vinegar, and stir well. Re-cover and continue to cook on the low-heat setting for 30 minutes to warm through and blend the flavors.

ASSEMBLE Using a large spoon, skim off and discard as much fat as possible from the surface of the picadillo. Taste and adjust the seasoning with salt.

SERVE Transfer to a serving dish and serve right away.

Thai Red Curry Beef

Keep coconut milk, prepared red curry paste, and Asian fish sauce on hand in the pantry for when the craving for Thai food strikes, then use them to create this luscious curry. The timing here is flexible, allowing you to customize it to your schedule. About 30 minutes before the curry is ready, start a pot of rice to serve with it.

ingredients

2½ lb (1.25 kg) boneless beef chuck, cut into 1½-inch (4-cm) pieces

Kosher salt and freshly ground pepper

3 tablespoons canola oil

1 yellow onion, finely chopped

4 cloves garlic, minced

¼ cup (2 oz/60 g) Thai red curry paste

2 cans (13½ fl oz/420 ml each) coconut milk, shaken well before opening

2 tablespoons Asian fish sauce

2 tablespoons fresh lime juice

2 tablespoons firmly packed dark brown sugar

3 tablespoons chopped fresh mint

makes 6–8 servings

step by step

PREP Season the beef with 1 teaspoon each salt and pepper.

BUILD FLAVOR (OPTIONAL) Put the slow-cooker insert on the stove top over medium-high heat, then add the oil and warm until hot. Working in batches if necessary to avoid crowding, add the beef and cook, turning frequently, until browned on all sides, about 10 minutes. Using a slotted spoon, transfer to a plate and set aside.

QUICK COOK If you have included the browning step, pour off all but 2 tablespoons of the fat from the insert and return the insert to medium-high heat. If you are starting here, put the slow-cooker insert on the stove top over medium-high heat, then add the oil and warm until hot. Add the onion and garlic and cook, stirring, for 1 minute. Add the curry paste and stir until it is fragrant and evenly coats the onion and garlic, about 30 seconds. Pour in the coconut milk and deglaze the insert, stirring and scraping up the browned bits on the insert bottom with a wooden spoon. Stir in the fish sauce, lime juice, and sugar and bring to a boil.

SLOW COOK Transfer the insert to the slow cooker and add the beef. Cover and cook on the high-heat setting for 3 hours or on the low-heat setting for 6 hours. The beef should be very tender and the sauce should be thick but still fluid.

SERVE Spoon the curry onto individual plates or into a large serving bowl. Sprinkle with the mint and serve right away.

Beef Pho

A big, steaming bowl of this Vietnamese beef noodle soup is perfect on a rainy day and remarkably simple to make at home. If you have homemade beef stock on hand, by all means, use it. I prefer skirt or flank steak for this recipe, both of which shred easily when cooked in the slow cooker until meltingly tender.

ingredients

8 cups (64 fl oz/2 l) low-sodium beef broth

1 yellow onion, halved and sliced

3 tablespoons Asian fish sauce

2 cinnamon sticks

4 star anise pods

2-inch (5-cm) piece fresh ginger, peeled and thinly sliced

½ teaspoon ground coriander

2 teaspoons sugar

Kosher salt

2 lb (1 kg) skirt or flank steak, cut into 4 equal pieces

¾ lb (375 g) dried rice noodles, about ⅛ inch (3 mm) wide

Bean sprouts, thinly sliced jalapeño chiles, lime wedges, fresh Thai basil, cilantro, and/or mint leaves, and Sriracha sauce for serving

makes 6 servings

step by step

SLOW COOK In the slow cooker, stir together the broth, onion, fish sauce, cinnamon, star anise, ginger, coriander, sugar, and 2 teaspoons salt. Add the steak, cover, and cook on the low-heat setting for 8 hours. The steak should be very tender.

ASSEMBLE Transfer the steak to a cutting board and shred into bite-size chunks with your fingers or 2 forks. Line a fine-mesh sieve with cheesecloth and strain the broth through the sieve into a bowl; discard the solids. Return the broth and the shredded steak to the slow cooker, cover, and cook on the low-heat setting for 30 minutes to warm through.

While the broth and meat are reheating, prepare the rice noodles according to package directions. Arrange the beans sprouts, chiles, lime wedges, and herbs on a platter and set on the table along with the Sriracha sauce.

SERVE Divide the rice noodles evenly among individual bowls and ladle the hot broth and steak over the noodles. Invite diners to top their soup with the herbs, sprouts, chiles, lime juice, and Sriracha as desired.

Red Wine Beef Stew

Hunks of beef braised slowly in red wine with sweet carrots, onions, and tomato are one of my favorite cool-weather main courses. Even if you have a small household, make a big batch of this stew; it freezes well. If you like, throw in some small red or white potatoes along with the tomatoes. Round out the meal with a big green salad.

ingredients

½ cup (2½ oz/75 g) all-purpose flour

Kosher salt and freshly ground pepper

3–4 lb (1.5–2 kg) boneless beef chuck, cut into 2-inch (5-cm) pieces

2 tablespoons unsalted butter

2 tablespoons canola oil

2 carrots, peeled and cut into 1-inch (2.5-cm) pieces

2 ribs celery, sliced

1 yellow onion, thinly sliced

1 lb (500 g) frozen pearl onions, thawed

1 teaspoon peppercorns

1 bottle (24 fl oz/750 ml) hearty red wine

1 can (28 oz/875 g) whole plum tomatoes, drained and chopped

1 cup (8 fl oz/250 ml) low-sodium beef broth

1 tablespoon tomato paste

makes 6–8 servings

step by step

PREP On a plate, stir together 3 tablespoons of the flour, 1 teaspoon salt, and 1 teaspoon pepper. Turn the beef pieces in the seasoned flour, coating evenly and shaking off any excess.

BUILD FLAVOR (OPTIONAL) Put the slow-cooker insert on the stove top over medium-high heat, then add the butter and oil and warm until hot. Working in batches if necessary to avoid crowding, cook the beef, turning frequently, until browned on all sides, about 10 minutes. Using a slotted spoon, transfer to a plate and set aside.

QUICK COOK If you have included the browning step, pour off all but ¼ cup (2 fl oz/60 ml) of the fat from the insert and return the insert to medium-high heat. If you are starting here, put the slow-cooker insert on the stove top over medium-high heat, then add the butter and oil and warm until hot. Add the carrots, celery, yellow onion, pearl onions, and peppercorns and cook, stirring often, until the onions and carrots begin to brown, about 5 minutes. Pour in the wine and deglaze the insert, stirring and scraping up the browned bits from the insert bottom with a wooden spoon. Stir in the tomatoes and broth and bring to a boil. Stir in the remaining 5 tablespoons (2 oz/60 g) flour and the tomato paste and cook, stirring frequently, until the mixture has thickened, about 1 minute.

SLOW COOK Transfer the insert to the slow cooker, add the beef, stir to mix well, and season the mixture with salt and pepper. Cover and cook on the low-heat setting for 4 hours. The meat should be very tender.

SERVE Spoon the stew into shallow individual bowls and serve right away.

Hot and Smoky Beef Chili

Chipotle chiles give this richly seasoned, stew-like chili a spicy-smoky flavor.
Set out your favorite chili toppings, such as sour cream, chopped green onions,
and shredded Cheddar cheese, so that diners can use them to personalize
their own portions at the table. Corn bread is the ideal accompaniment.

ingredients

2 tablespoons olive oil

1 yellow onion, chopped

2 cloves garlic, minced

3 lb (1.5 kg) boneless beef chuck,
cut into ¼-inch (6-mm) cubes

2 tablespoons chile powder

1 teaspoon ground cumin

3 tomatoes, seeded and chopped

2 chipotle chiles in adobo sauce, chopped

1 jalapeño chile, seeded and chopped

1 tablespoon tomato paste

1 cup (8 fl oz/250 ml) low-sodium
beef broth

1 cup (8 fl oz/250 ml) dark beer

1 can (15 oz/470 g) red kidney beans,
drained and rinsed

Kosher salt and freshly ground pepper

makes 6—8 servings

step by step

QUICK COOK Put the slow-cooker insert on the stove top over medium-high heat, then add the oil and warm until hot. Add the onion and cook, stirring, until softened, 3—5 minutes. Add the garlic and cook, stirring, for 1 minute. Working in batches if necessary to avoid crowding, add the beef and cook, turning as needed, until browned on all sides, about 10 minutes. Stir in the chile powder and cumin and cook, stirring frequently, until fragrant, about 2 minutes.

SLOW COOK Transfer the insert to the slow cooker and add the tomatoes, chipotle chiles, jalapeño chile, tomato paste, broth, beer, and beans. Season with salt and pepper and stir well. Cover and cook on the low-heat setting for 8 hours. The beef should be very tender. If the sauce is too thin, uncover and cook on the high-heat setting for up to 30 minutes.

SERVE Spoon the chili into bowls and serve right away.

Korean Beef
and
Kimchi Stew

Kimchi and gochujang—a spicy, slightly sweet Korean hot-pepper paste—infuse this stew with authentic Korean flavor and plenty of umami. You can find gochujang at many well-stocked markets or Asian markets. Serve lots of steamed rice alongside.

ingredients

2 tablespoons canola oil

4 lb (2 kg) English-cut beef short ribs

Kosher salt and freshly ground pepper

1 red onion, finely chopped

1 carrot, peeled and finely chopped

1 tablespoon minced garlic

1 tablespoon peeled and minced fresh ginger

¼ cup (1½ oz/45 g) all-purpose flour

1 cup (8 fl oz/250 ml) low-sodium chicken broth

½ cup (8 fl oz/250ml) low-sodium soy sauce

½ cup (2½ oz/75 g) kimchi

¼ cup (2 oz/60 g) gochujang

¼ cup (2 oz/60 g) firmly packed dark brown sugar

Sliced green onions (white and pale green parts) and toasted sesame seeds for garnish

makes 4–6 servings

step by step

BUILD FLAVOR (OPTIONAL) Put the slow-cooker insert on the stove top over medium-high heat, then add the oil and warm until hot. Add half of the ribs and cook, turning as needed, until evenly browned, 10–12 minutes. Using tongs, transfer to a plate. Repeat with the remaining ribs, add to the plate, and set aside.

QUICK COOK If you have included the browning step, pour off all but about 2 tablespoons of the fat from the insert and return the insert to medium-high heat. If you are starting here, put the slow-cooker insert on the stove top over medium-high heat, then add the oil and warm until hot. Add the onion, carrot, garlic, and ginger and cook, stirring, until softened, about 5 minutes. Whisk in the flour and cook, stirring, until fully corporated, 30–60 seconds. Pour in the broth and soy sauce. Add the kimchi, ochujang, sugar, and ½ teaspoon salt, and stir well. Bring the liquid to a boil.

SLOW COOK Transfer the insert to the slow cooker and add the ribs, submerging them in the liquid. Cover and cook on the low-heat setting for 7 hours. The meat should be tender.

ASSEMBLE Transfer the ribs to a platter and cover to keep warm. Using a large spoon, skim off and discard as much fat as possible from the surface of the cooking liquid.

SERVE Spoon the cooking liquid over the ribs, garnish with green onions and sesame seeds, and serve right away.

Beef and Squash Curry
with
Coconut Milk

This Thai-inspired curry would also be delicious with red or even yellow curry paste, so you can customize it to suit the tastes of your household. If you like it spicy, add some minced bird's eye or jalapeño chile along with the onion and garlic. Serve the stew with steamed jasmine rice; stir in a little chopped cilantro or toasted coconut if you like.

ingredients

1 tablespoon canola oil

1 yellow onion, chopped

2 cloves garlic, minced

¼ cup (2 oz/60 g) green curry paste

3 tablespoons all-purpose flour

2 tablespoons tomato paste

1 can (13½ ounces/420 ml) coconut milk, shaken well before opening

1 cup (8 fl oz/250 ml) low-sodium chicken broth

3 tablespoons fresh lime juice

3 tablespoons golden brown sugar

2 tablespoons Asian fish sauce

Kosher salt and freshly ground pepper

2 lb (1 kg) boneless beef chuck, cut into 1½-inch (4-cm) pieces

3 cups (15 oz/470 g) peeled and cubed butternut squash (1½-inch/4-cm cubes)

Chopped fresh cilantro for garnish (optional)

makes 6 servings

step by step

QUICK COOK Put the slow-cooker insert on the stove top over medium-high heat, then add the oil and warm until hot. Add the onion and garlic and cook, stirring, until beginning to soften, about 3 minutes. Whisk in the curry paste, flour, and tomato paste and cook, stirring, until the flour is fully incorporated, about 1 minute. Add the coconut milk, broth, lime juice, sugar, fish sauce, 1 teaspoon salt, and a few grinds of pepper, stir well, and bring to a boil.

SLOW COOK Transfer the insert to the slow cooker, add the beef and squash, and stir to mix, arranging the squash on the bottom. Cover and cook on the low-heat setting for 6 hours. The beef and squash should both be tender.

SERVE Using a large spoon, skim off any fat from the surface of the curry. Transfer the curry to a serving bowl, garnish with cilantro, if desired, and serve right away.

Beef Adobo

This version of adobo, the popular Philippine specialty seasoned with vinegar, soy sauce, and garlic, calls for beef shanks, the bones of which impart extra flavor and body to the dish. The meat is shredded from the bones, then rolled up in lettuce leaves along with fresh mango salsa and eaten like a taco. Accompany with steamed rice, if you like.

ingredients

5 lb (2.5 kg) meaty beef shanks, cut into ½-inch- (12-mm-) wide pieces by the butcher

Kosher salt and freshly ground pepper

2 tablespoons peanut oil

1 yellow onion, finely chopped

1 large carrot, peeled and finely chopped

10 cloves garlic, smashed

3 bay leaves

4 star anise pods

1 cup (8 fl oz/250 ml) rice vinegar

½ cup (4 fl oz/125 ml) low-sodium soy sauce

2 hearts of romaine lettuce, leaves separated

Purchased mango salsa for serving

makes 4–6 servings

step by step

PREP Lightly season the beef shanks with salt and pepper.

BUILD FLAVOR (OPTIONAL) Put the slow-cooker insert on the stove top over medium-high heat, then add the oil and warm until hot. Working in batches if necessary to avoid crowding, add the shanks and sear, turning as needed, until browned on all sides, about 8 minutes. Using tongs, transfer the shanks to a plate and set aside.

QUICK COOK If you have included the browning step, pour off all but 2 tablespoons of the fat from the insert and return the insert to medium-high heat. If you are starting here, put the slow-cooker insert on the stove top over medium-high heat, then add the oil and warm until hot. Add the onion and carrot and cook, stirring, until softened and just beginning to brown, about 6 minutes. Add the garlic, bay leaves, and star anise and cook, stirring, for 1 minute. Pour in the vinegar and soy sauce and deglaze the insert, stirring and scraping up the browned bits on the insert bottom with a wooden spoon. Bring to a boil.

SLOW COOK Transfer the insert to the slow cooker and add the shanks in an even layer. Cover and cook on the low-heat setting for 8 hours, basting the meat with the braising liquid two or three times if possible. The beef should be very tender.

ASSEMBLE Transfer the beef shanks to a plate and cover to keep warm. Strain the cooking liquid through a fine-mesh sieve into a small saucepan. Retrieve the garlic cloves from the sieve and discard the remaining solids. Let the liquid stand for a few minutes, then, using a large spoon, skim off and discard as much fat as possible. Using a fork, smash the garlic cloves into a paste and stir them into the liquid. Put the pan over high heat, bring to a rapid simmer, and cook until slightly reduced, about 5 minutes. Meanwhile, remove the meat from the bones and discard the bones and any large pieces of fat. Shred the meat with 2 forks. Moisten the meat with the reduced liquid.

SERVE Arrange the lettuce leaves on a platter or individual plates. Spoon the meat over or alongside the lettuce leaves, top with the salsa, and serve right away.

Shredded Beef Ragù
with
Egg Noodles

This pasta topped with luscious, shredded meat sauce gets a lift with the addition of anchovy and black olives. If you make it in the summer months, substitute 3 or 4 seeded and chopped juicy, ripe tomatoes for the canned tomatoes. For a different spin, omit the egg noodles and serve the ragù over soft polenta.

ingredients

2 tablespoons olive oil

3 lb (1.5 kg) boneless beef chuck, cut into ¼-inch (6-mm) pieces

1 yellow onion, chopped

1 clove garlic, minced

1 teaspoon anchovy paste

1 tablespoon chopped fresh oregano, or 1 teaspoon dried

1 can (28 oz/875 g) crushed tomatoes with juice

1 cup (8 fl oz/250 ml) low-sodium beef broth

½ cup (2 oz/60 g) pitted black olives, halved

½ teaspoon red pepper flakes

Kosher salt and freshly ground pepper

1 lb (500 g) fresh or dried wide egg noodles

makes 4–6 servings

step by step

BUILD FLAVOR (OPTIONAL) Put the slow-cooker insert on the stove top over medium heat, then add the oil and warm until hot. Working in batches if necessary to avoid crowding, add the beef and cook, stirring occasionally, until no longer pink, about 10 minutes. Using a slotted spoon, transfer to a plate and set aside.

QUICK COOK If you have included the browning step, pour off all but 2 tablespoons of the fat from the insert and return the insert to medium-high heat. If you are starting here, put the slow-cooker insert on the stove top over medium-high heat, then add the oil and warm until hot. Add the onion and cook, stirring, until softened, 3–5 minutes. Stir in the garlic, anchovy paste, and oregano and cook, stirring, for 1 minute longer. Stir in the tomatoes and their juice and the broth and bring to a boil.

SLOW COOK Transfer the insert to the slow cooker, add the beef, and stir to coat evenly with the vegetable mixture. Cover and cook on the low-heat setting for 4 hours. The beef should be very tender and the flavors blended.

Uncover and stir in the olives and pepper flakes. Re-cover and cook on the low-heat setting just until warmed through, 10–15 minutes. Season with salt and pepper.

ASSEMBLE About 15 minutes before the ragù is ready, bring a large pot three-fourths full of water to a boil. Add 2 tablespoons salt and the noodles and cook until al dente, according to the package directions. Drain the noodles and return to the pot. Add about ½ cup (4 fl oz/125 ml) of the ragù and toss gently to coat.

SERVE Divide the noodles among shallow individual bowls and top with additional ragù. Serve right away.

Classic Bolognese
with
Fresh Pappardelle

A true Bolognese sauce lends itself to long slow cooking at a low temperature, making the slow cooker a perfect vehicle for making a thick, luscious sauce. Bacon adds a smoky aroma, and a small amount of milk keeps the meat succulent. Serve half of the sauce for dinner tonight and freeze the rest for a last-minute weeknight treat.

ingredients

3 thick slices applewood-smoked bacon or pancetta, finely diced

1 large yellow onion, finely diced

2 carrots, peeled and finely diced

2 ribs celery, finely diced

Kosher salt and freshly ground pepper

2 cloves garlic, minced

1½ lb (750 g) lean ground beef

1½ lb (750 g) ground pork shoulder

½ cup (4 fl oz/125 ml) whole milk

1 can (28 oz/875 g) crushed tomatoes with juice

2 cups (16 fl oz/500 ml) low-sodium beef broth

1 cup (8 fl oz/250 ml) full-bodied red wine

1 lb (500 g) fresh pappardelle or fettuccine

½ cup (2 oz/60 g) freshly shaved or grated Parmesan cheese

makes 4–6 servings, plus leftover sauce

step by step

QUICK COOK Put the slow-cooker insert on the stove top over medium-high heat, then add the bacon. Fry the bacon, stirring, until crisp. Add the onion, carrots, celery, 1 teaspoon salt, and a few grinds of pepper and cook, stirring, until softened, about 8 minutes. Stir in the garlic, then stir in the beef and pork and cook, stirring and breaking up the meats with a wooden spoon, until they are no longer pink, about 5 minutes. Stir in the milk and cook for 2 minutes. Pour in the tomatoes and wine and stir until blended. Bring the sauce just to a boil.

SLOW COOK Transfer the insert to the slow cooker. Cover and cook on the low-heat setting for 8–10 hours. The sauce should be thick and the flavors blended. Taste and adjust the seasoning with salt and pepper.

ASSEMBLE About 15 minutes before the sauce is ready, bring a large pot three-fourths full of water to a boil. Add 2 tablespoons salt and the pasta and cook until al dente, 2–4 minutes or according to the package directions. Drain the pasta and return to the pot. Add about ½ cup (4 fl oz/125 ml) of the sauce and toss gently to coat.

SERVE Divide the pasta among shallow individual bowls and top with additional sauce. Sprinkle a little of the Parmesan over each serving and serve right away. Pass the remaining cheese at the table.

Ropa Vieja

Don't let the name of this classic Cuban dish—"old clothes"—put you off. The beef emerges from the slow cooker succulent and flavorful. I like to serve this delicious, simple-to-put-together concoction with steamed rice or mashed or roasted potatoes.

ingredients

1 cup (8 fl oz/250 ml) low-sodium beef broth

1 can (15 oz/470 g) crushed tomatoes with juice

1 tablespoon tomato paste

1 yellow onion, finely chopped

1 small green bell pepper, seeded and finely chopped

1 small red bell pepper, seeded and finely chopped

3 cloves garlic, minced

2 teaspoons ground cumin

2 teaspoons dried oregano

1 tablespoon sugar

Kosher salt and freshly ground pepper

3 lb (1.5 kg) flank steak, cut into 6 equal pieces

½ cup (2½ oz/75 g) pitted and sliced green olives

⅓ cup (½ oz/15 g) chopped fresh cilantro, plus small sprigs for garnish (optional)

3 tablespoons cider vinegar

makes 6—8 servings

step by step

SLOW COOK In the slow cooker, combine the broth, tomatoes, tomato paste, onion, green and red bell peppers, garlic, cumin, oregano, and sugar and stir to mix well. Generously salt the steak and add it to the slow cooker, nestling the pieces in the sauce. Cover and cook on the low-heat setting for 8 hours. The meat should be very tender.

ASSEMBLE Transfer the meat to a cutting board. Using 2 forks, shred into medium-size pieces. Using a large spoon, skim off and discard any fat from the surface of the cooking liquid. Return the meat to the slow cooker, add the olives, chopped cilantro, and vinegar, and stir to mix well. Taste and adjust the seasoning with more vinegar, salt, and pepper. Cover and cook on the low-heat setting for 30 minutes to warm through.

SERVE Transfer the meat mixture with the sauce to a platter, garnish with cilantro, if using, and serve right away.

Beef Stew
with
Mushrooms and Barley

Slightly chewy barley contributes great texture to this long-cooked beef and root vegetable dish. The liquid from rehydrating dried porcini mushrooms becomes part of the savory sauce, adding a nice depth of flavor. Chopped herbs sprinkled on top at the end lend a welcome fresh accent to the long-simmered dish.

ingredients

1 oz (30 g) dried porcini mushrooms

2 cups (16 fl oz/500 ml) boiling water

2 tablespoons unsalted butter

2 lb (1 kg) boneless beef chuck, cut into 2-inch (5-cm) pieces

2 yellow onions, finely chopped

2 cloves garlic, minced

1 lb (500 g) fresh cremini mushrooms, brushed clean and thinly sliced

2 cups (16 fl oz/500 ml) low-sodium beef broth

½ cup (3½ oz/105 g) pearled barley

3 carrots, finely chopped

2 parsnips, peeled and finely chopped

Kosher salt and freshly ground pepper

2 tablespoons chopped fresh dill or flat-leaf parsley

makes 4–6 servings

step by step

PREP Put the dried mushrooms in a heatproof bowl, add the boiling water, and let soak for 20 minutes. Line a fine-mesh sieve with a double layer of cheesecloth, place over a bowl, and drain the mushrooms in the sieve. Set the captured soaking liquid aside. Rinse the mushrooms under cold running water, then chop finely. Set the mushrooms aside.

QUICK COOK Put the slow-cooker insert on the stove top over medium-high heat, then add the butter and warm until melted. Working in batches if necessary to avoid crowding, add the beef and cook, turning as needed, until browned on all sides, about 10 minutes. Transfer the beef to a plate and set aside.

Add the onion to the insert and cook over medium-high heat, stirring, until softened, 3–5 minutes. Add the garlic and cook, stirring, for 1 minute. Lower the heat to medium, add the rehydrated mushrooms and the fresh mushrooms, and sauté until they start to brown and release their liquid, about 5 minutes. Stir in the mushroom soaking liquid and the broth and bring to a boil.

SLOW COOK Transfer the insert to the slow cooker, add the beef, and stir to coat evenly with the mushroom mixture. Cover and cook on the low-heat setting for 3 hours.

Uncover and stir in the barley and ½ cup (4 fl oz/125 ml) water. Re-cover and cook on the low-heat setting for 2 hours. Uncover and stir in the carrots and parsnips. Re-cover and cook on the low-heat setting for 1 hour longer. The beef, barley, and vegetables should be tender. Season with salt and pepper.

SERVE Spoon the stew into individual bowls, garnish with the dill, and serve right away.

Beef Goulash
with
Bacon and Potatoes

Sweet paprika and caraway are the foundation of this Hungarian-style stew,
so make sure you have a fresh supply of the spices. Serve this hearty dish
like I do, and as they do in Hungary, spooned over buttered egg noodles with
a big dollop of sour cream and a sprinkle of chopped fresh flat-leaf parsley.

ingredients

2 lb (1 kg) boneless beef chuck, cut into 2-inch (5-cm) pieces

Kosher salt and freshly ground pepper

1 tablespoon canola oil

4 slices bacon, about ¼ lb (125 g) total weight

2 yellow onions, chopped

2 cloves garlic, minced

1 tablespoon sweet paprika

1 teaspoon caraway seeds

5 sprigs fresh oregano

1 tablespoon tomato paste

1 cup (8 fl oz/250 ml) dry white wine

1 cup (8 fl oz/250 ml) low-sodium chicken broth

1 red bell pepper, seeded and chopped

6 Yukon gold potatoes, about 2 lb (1 kg) total weight, quartered

½ cup (4 oz/125 g) sour cream

Chopped fresh flat-leaf parsley for garnish

makes 4–6 servings

step by step

PREP Season the beef generously with salt and pepper.

BUILD FLAVOR (OPTIONAL) Put the slow-cooker insert on the stove top over medium-high heat, then add the oil and warm until hot. Working in batches if necessary to avoid crowding, add the beef and cook, turning as needed, until browned on all sides, about 10 minutes. Using a slotted spoon, transfer to a plate and set aside.

QUICK COOK If you have included the browning step, pour off all but 1 tablespoon of the fat from the insert and return the insert to medium-high heat. If you are starting here, put the slow-cooker insert on the stove top over medium-high heat, then add the oil and warm until hot. Add the bacon and cook, turning frequently, until crisp, about 5 minutes. Transfer the bacon to paper towels to drain. When the bacon is cool, chop coarsely and set aside.

Pour off all but 2 tablespoons of the fat from the insert and return the insert to medium-high heat. Add the onions and cook, stirring, until softened, 3–5 minutes. Add the garlic and cook, stirring, for 1 minute. Stir in the paprika, caraway, oregano, tomato paste, wine, and broth and bring to a boil.

SLOW COOK Transfer the insert to the slow cooker, add the beef, and stir to combine evenly with the broth mixture. Cover and cook on the low-heat setting for 6 hours. Uncover and stir in the reserved bacon, the bell pepper, and the potatoes. Re-cover and continue to cook on the low-heat setting for 2 hours longer. The beef and the potatoes should be fork-tender and the sauce should be thick. Season with salt and pepper.

SERVE Spoon the goulash into individual bowls and garnish with the sour cream and parsley. Serve right away.

Beer-Braised Corned Beef *and* Winter Vegetables

A cinch to prepare, this stick-to-your-ribs dish is ideal for both a special occasion and a cozy family supper. Offer thick slices of warm, buttered rye bread and pints of full-bodied ale. If you plan to prepare this dish in advance, be sure to save the defatted braising liquid for drizzling over the meat before reheating.

ingredients

1 point-cut corned beef brisket with juices and enclosed spice packet, about 3 lb (1.5 kg)

1 red onion, chopped

⅓ cup (2 oz/60 g) drained sauerkraut

¼ cup (2 oz/60 g) prepared yellow mustard

1 tablespoon golden brown sugar

Kosher salt and freshly ground pepper

1½ cups (12 fl oz/375 ml) brown or red ale

1 cup (8 fl oz/250 ml) low-sodium chicken broth

1½ lb (750 g) small yellow or white potatoes, halved or quartered if large

4 carrots, peeled and cut into 2-inch (5-cm) lengths

1 small green cabbage, cut into 6—8 wedges through the stem end

makes 6—8 servings

step by step

PREP Put the brisket and juices and the contents of the spice packet in the slow-cooker insert. Add the onion, sauerkraut, mustard, sugar, 1 teaspoon salt, and a few grinds of pepper and mix well with your hands. Pour in the beer and broth.

SLOW COOK Transfer the insert to the slow cooker, cover, and cook on the low-heat setting for 6 hours. The brisket and vegetables should be very tender.

Uncover and add the potatoes, carrots, and cabbage wedges, submerging them in the liquid. Re-cover and continue to cook on the low-heat setting for 2 hours. The vegetables and brisket should be very tender.

ASSEMBLE Transfer the brisket to a cutting board. Tent with aluminum foil and let rest for 5 minutes. Using a large, sharp knife, cut the brisket across the grain into thin slices. If you wish to serve the braising liquid, using a large spoon, skim off and discard as much fat as possible from the surface of the liquid.

SERVE Divide the sliced corned beef and vegetables among 4 plates. If desired, spoon some of the warm braising liquid over each serving. Serve right away.

Short Ribs
with
Red Wine and Balsamic

I love these short ribs. Rich and indulgent, they are special enough for an
I-want-to-impress-someone dinner, but simple enough to make midweek.
Leftovers can be shredded, mixed with the sauce, warmed, and served over pasta.

ingredients

3 tablespoons all-purpose flour

Kosher salt and freshly ground pepper

5½–6 lb (2.75–3 kg) English-cut beef
short ribs

¼ cup (2 fl oz/60 ml) olive oil

2 oz (60 g) pancetta, chopped

2 yellow onions, finely chopped

4 cloves garlic, minced

1 teaspoon red pepper flakes

2 carrots, peeled and chopped

2 tablespoons tomato paste

1 tablespoon sugar

1 cup (8 fl oz/250 ml) dry red wine

1 can (14½ oz/455 g) diced plum tomatoes
with juice

1 cup (8 fl oz/250 ml) low-sodium
beef broth

¼ cup (2 fl oz/60 ml) balsamic vinegar

2 bay leaves

2 sprigs fresh rosemary

2 sprigs fresh thyme

1 tablespoon dried oregano

makes 6–8 servings

step by step

PREP On a plate, stir together the flour, 1 teaspoon salt, and ½ teaspoon
pepper. Turn the ribs in the seasoned flour, coating evenly and shaking
off any excess.

BUILD FLAVOR (OPTIONAL) Put the slow-cooker insert on the stove
top over medium-high heat, then add the oil and warm until hot. Working
in batches to avoid crowding, add the short ribs and cook, turning as
needed, until evenly browned, 10–12 minutes. Using tongs, transfer to
a plate and set aside.

QUICK COOK If you have included the browning step, pour off all but
¼ cup (2 fl oz/60 ml) of the fat from the insert and return the insert to
medium-high heat. If you are starting here, put the slow-cooker insert
on the stove top over medium-high heat, then add the oil and warm until
hot. Add the pancetta and cook, stirring often, until most of the fat is
rendered, about 5 minutes. Add the onions and cook, stirring, until just
beginning to soften, about 3 minutes. Stir in the garlic and pepper flakes
and cook, stirring, until fragrant, about 30 seconds. Add the carrots,
tomato paste, and sugar and cook, stirring frequently, until well blended,
about 1 minute. Add the wine and deglaze the insert, stirring and scraping
up the browned bits on the insert bottom with a wooden spoon. Bring
the wine to a boil, then stir in the tomatoes, broth, and balsamic vinegar;
return to a boil.

SLOW COOK Transfer the insert to the slow cooker, add the ribs, bay
leaves, rosemary, thyme, and oregano, and toss the ribs to coat evenly
with the tomato sauce. Cover and cook on the low-heat setting for 6 hours.
The meat should be fork-tender and easy to pull from the bone.

ASSEMBLE When the ribs are ready, transfer to a platter and cover
to keep warm. Remove and discard the rosemary and thyme sprigs and
the bay leaves. Using a large spoon, skim off and discard as much fat
as possible from the surface of the cooking liquid. Season lightly with
salt and pepper.

SERVE Transfer the ribs to individual plates, spoon the cooking liquid
over and around them, and serve right away.

Braised Short Ribs
with
Lemongrass, Ginger, and Hoisin

The dark sweetness of hoisin sauce along with the bright sparkle of ginger, lemongrass, and rice vinegar impart robust flavor to these succulent ribs. Serve them with fragrant jasmine rice and a cucumber salad dressed with seasoned rice vinegar.

ingredients

3 tablespoons all-purpose flour

Kosher salt and freshly ground pepper

5½–6 lb (2.75–3 kg) flanken-cut beef short ribs

¼ cup (2 fl oz/60 ml) canola oil

4 cloves garlic, minced

4 green onions, white and pale green parts, thinly sliced

2 tablespoons peeled and minced fresh ginger

1 teaspoon red pepper flakes

2 stalks lemongrass, tender bulb part only, trimmed, halved lengthwise, and crushed with a meat pounder

1 cup (8 fl oz/250 ml) low-sodium beef broth

½ cup (4 fl oz/125 ml) low-sodium soy sauce

½ cup (4 fl oz/125 ml) hoisin sauce

½ cup (4 fl oz/125 ml) rice vinegar

½ cup (3½ oz/105 g) firmly packed dark brown sugar

¼ cup (2 fl oz/60 ml) Sriracha sauce

makes 6–8 servings

step by step

PREP On a plate, stir together the flour, 1 teaspoon salt, and ½ teaspoon pepper. Turn the short ribs in the seasoned flour, coating evenly and shaking off any excess.

BUILD FLAVOR (OPTIONAL) Put the slow-cooker insert on the stove top over medium-high heat, then add the oil and warm until hot. Working in batches to avoid crowding, add the short ribs and cook, turning as needed, until evenly browned, 10–12 minutes. Using tongs, transfer to a plate and set aside.

QUICK COOK If you have included the browning step, pour off all but ¼ cup (2 fl oz/60 ml) of the fat from the insert and return the insert to medium-high heat. If you are starting here, put the slow-cooker insert on the stove top over medium-high heat, then add the oil and warm until hot. Add the garlic, green onions, ginger, pepper flakes, and lemongrass and cook, stirring, until fragrant, about 1 minute. Pour in the beef broth and deglaze the insert, stirring and scraping up the browned bits on the insert bottom with a wooden spoon. Stir in the soy sauce, hoisin sauce, vinegar, sugar, and Sriracha sauce and bring to a boil.

SLOW COOK Transfer the insert to the slow cooker, add the ribs, and spoon the broth mixture over the ribs to coat evenly. Cover and cook on the low-heat setting for 6 hours. The ribs should be fork-tender.

ASSEMBLE Transfer the ribs to a platter and cover to keep warm. Remove and discard the lemongrass from the braising liquid. Using a large spoon, skim off and discard as much fat as possible from the surface of the braising liquid.

SERVE Divide the ribs among individual plates, spoon the braising liquid over and around them, and serve right away.

Home-Style Pot Roast

I use two sets of vegetables in this stew. The first set—carrots, yellow onion, and celery—flavor the meat for 8 hours while it cooks. The second set—potatoes, pearl onions, peas, and more carrots—simmers with the beef for only one hour, so the vegetables retain their bright color, distinctive texture, and fresh taste. To save time, prep all of the vegetables the night before you plan to cook and store them in the refrigerator. Accompany the pot roast with a simple green salad and crusty bread.

ingredients

5 tablespoons (2 oz/60 g) all-purpose flour

Kosher salt and freshly ground pepper

1 boneless beef chuck roast, 3–4 lb (1.5–2 kg)

2 tablespoons unsalted butter, if including the optional browning step

2 tablespoons canola oil

4 carrots, 2 peeled and finely chopped and 2 peeled and cut into 1-inch (2.5-cm) pieces

1 yellow onion, chopped

1 rib celery, chopped

3 cups (24 fl oz/750 ml) low-sodium beef broth

3 Yukon gold potatoes, about 1 lb (500 g) total weight, peeled and quartered

1 cup (6 oz/185 g) frozen pearl onions

½ cup (2½ oz/75 g) frozen English peas

makes 6 servings

step by step

PREP In a large bowl, stir together 3 tablespoons of the flour, 1 teaspoon salt, and ½ teaspoon pepper. Turn the roast in the seasoned flour, coating evenly and shaking off any excess.

BUILD FLAVOR (OPTIONAL) Put the slow-cooker insert on the stove top over medium-high heat, then add the butter and oil and warm until hot. Add the roast and cook, turning as needed, until browned on all sides, about 10 minutes. Transfer to a plate and set aside.

QUICK COOK If you have included the browning step, pour off all but 2 tablespoons of the fat from the insert and return the insert to medium-high heat. If you are starting here, put the slow-cooker insert on the stove top over medium-high heat, then add the oil and warm until hot. Add the chopped carrots, yellow onion, and celery and cook, stirring, until softened, about 5 minutes. Stir in the remaining 2 tablespoons flour and cook, stirring, until fully incorporated, about 1 minute. Pour in the broth and deglaze the insert, stirring and scraping up the browned bits on the insert bottom with a wooden spoon. Bring to a boil.

SLOW COOK Transfer the insert to the slow cooker, add the roast, and spoon the broth and vegetable mixture evenly over the roast. Cover and cook on the low-heat setting for 8 hours.

Transfer the roast to a large plate. Strain the cooking liquid through a fine-mesh sieve into a heatproof bowl and discard the solids. Using a large spoon, skim off and discard as much fat as possible from the surface of the cooking liquid. Return the roast and cooking liquid to the slow cooker and stir in the potatoes, carrot pieces, and pearl onions. Cover and cook on the low-heat setting for 45 minutes. Uncover and stir in the peas. Re-cover and continue to cook on the low-heat setting for about 15 minutes longer. The vegetables should be tender.

ASSEMBLE Transfer the roast to a cutting board, tent with aluminum foil, and let rest for 5 minutes. Re-cover the cooker to keep the vegetables and cooking liquid warm. Using a large, sharp knife, slice the roast across the grain.

SERVE Divide the slices evenly among individual plates. Using a large spoon, divide the vegetables and cooking liquid evenly among the plates. Season with salt and pepper and serve right away.

Tangy Braised Brisket

When buying beef brisket, you can choose between a flat cut and a point cut. The flat cut is leaner and easier to slice, but the point cut is more succulent because it contains more fat and braises beautifully in a slow cooker; I recommend choosing the point cut whenever you plan to slow cook a brisket. Serve with coleslaw or potato salad.

ingredients

¼ cup (2 oz/60 g) firmly packed dark brown sugar

¼ cup (2 fl oz/60 ml) cider vinegar

2 tomatoes, seeded and chopped

2 cups (16 fl oz/500 ml) low-sodium beef broth

1 beef brisket, about 3 lb (1.5 kg), trimmed of excess fat

Kosher salt and freshly ground pepper

2 tablespoons canola oil

2 yellow onions, thinly sliced

2 cloves garlic, minced

½ teaspoon ground allspice

2 tablespoons all-purpose flour

makes 6—8 servings

step by step

PREP In a small bowl, stir together the sugar, vinegar, tomatoes, and broth. Set aside. Season the brisket generously with salt and pepper.

BUILD FLAVOR (OPTIONAL) Put the slow-cooker insert on the stove top over medium-high heat, then add the oil and warm until hot. Add the brisket, fat side down, and cook, turning once, until browned on both sides, about 10 minutes total. Transfer to a plate and set aside.

QUICK COOK If you have included the browning step, pour off all but 2 tablespoons of the fat from the insert and return the insert to medium-high heat. If you are starting here, put the slow-cooker insert on the stove top over medium-high heat, then add the oil and warm until hot. Add the onions and cook, stirring, until softened, about 3 minutes. Add the garlic and cook, stirring, until fragrant, about 1 minute. Stir in the allspice, then sprinkle the flour evenly over the onion mixture. Turn down the heat to medium and cook, stirring frequently, until the flour is fully incorporated, about 3 minutes. Pour in the reserved broth mixture and stir to combine. Bring to a boil and season with salt and pepper.

SLOW COOK Transfer the insert to the slow cooker, add the brisket, and spoon the broth and onion mixture over the meat. Cover and cook on the low-heat setting for 6—8 hours. The brisket should be very tender.

Using a large spoon, skim off and discard as much fat as possible from the braising liquid. Let the brisket rest, uncovered, in the liquid for 1—2 hours.

ASSEMBLE Transfer the brisket to a cutting board. Using a large, sharp knife, cut the brisket across the grain into thin slices. In a saucepan over medium heat, warm the braising liquid.

SERVE Arrange the slices on a platter, top with the hot braising liquid, and serve right away.

Sauerbraten

Perfect a cold autumn evening, this adaptation of a traditional German recipe is a combination of sweet, sour, and savory flavors. Gingersnaps may seem like an unlikely ingredient, but they add intriguing spiciness to the dish and help thicken the sauce. Serve with boiled red potatoes tossed with butter and herbs.

ingredients

1 boneless beef chuck roast, 3½–4 lb (1.75–2 kg)

Kosher salt and freshly ground pepper

1 teaspoon ground ginger

1 cup (8 fl oz/250 ml) low-sodium beef broth

¾ cup (6 fl oz/180 ml) cider vinegar

½ cup (3½ oz/105 g) firmly packed dark brown sugar

2 yellow onions, chopped

1 bay leaf

½ head red cabbage, halved lengthwise, cored, and thinly shredded crosswise

12–16 gingersnap cookies, finely crushed

makes 8 servings

step by step

PREP Season the roast generously with salt and pepper. Sprinkle with the ground ginger, then pat the seasonings into the meat.

QUICK COOK Put the slow-cooker insert on the stove top over high heat, then pour in the broth and vinegar and bring to a boil. Add the brown sugar and stir until it dissolves. Add the onions and bay leaf and remove from the heat.

SLOW COOK Transfer the insert to the slow cooker, add the roast, and spoon the broth mixture evenly over and around the roast. Cover and cook on the low-heat setting for 7 hours.

Sprinkle the cabbage evenly with 1 teaspoon salt, then uncover the cooker and tuck the cabbage around the roast, pressing it down into the liquid. Re-cover and continue to cook on the low-heat setting for 1 hour longer.

ASSEMBLE Transfer the roast to a cutting board, tent with aluminum foil, and let rest for 10 minutes. Using a slotted spoon, transfer the cabbage to a serving bowl and cover to keep warm. Remove and discard the bay leaf from the cooking liquid. Using a large spoon, skim off and discard as much fat as possible from the surface of the liquid. Stir enough of the gingersnaps into the liquid to form a thick sauce, then season with salt and pepper. Using a large, sharp knife, cut the meat across the grain into thick slices.

SERVE Divide the meat slices and cabbage evenly among individual plates. Spoon the gravy on top and serve right away.

Spiced Lamb Ragù
with
Fresh Pasta

A heady mix of herbs and spices—coriander, fennel, cumin, rosemary—gives
this substantial sauce memorable flavor. If you cannot find fresh pappardelle,
fresh or dried fettuccine or even a dried tube pasta, such as rigatoni,
can be substituted. Serve with broccolini that has been boiled just until
crisp-tender, then seared in a hot frying pan with garlic, olive oil, and lemon juice.

ingredients

1 tablespoon olive oil

3 tablespoons unsalted butter

1 carrot, peeled and finely chopped

1 yellow onion, finely chopped

1 rib celery, finely chopped

1 teaspoon minced garlic

1½ lb (750 g) ground lamb

1 teaspoon ground coriander

1 teaspoon ground fennel

1 teaspoon ground cumin

2 teaspoons minced fresh rosemary

¼ teaspoon red pepper flakes

½ cup (4 fl oz/125 ml) dry red wine

2 tablespoons tomato paste

2 cups (16 fl oz/500 ml) strained tomatoes

1 cup (8 fl oz/250 ml) low-sodium
chicken broth

Kosher salt and freshly ground pepper

1 lb (500 g) fresh pappardelle

½ cup (2 oz/60 g) freshly shaved or grated
Parmesan cheese

makes 4–6 servings

step by step

QUICK COOK Put the slow-cooker insert on the stove top over medium-high heat, then add the oil and 1 tablespoon of the butter and warm until the butter is melted. Add the carrot, onion, celery, and garlic and cook, stirring, until softened, 5 minutes. Add the lamb, coriander, fennel, cumin, 1 teaspoon of the rosemary, and the pepper flakes and cook, stirring and breaking up the lamb with a wooden spoon, until the lamb is no longer pink, 5–8 minutes. Stir in the wine and tomato paste and simmer until the wine evaporates, about 3 minutes. Pour in the tomatoes and broth, add 1½ teaspoons salt and a few grinds of pepper, stir well, and bring to a boil.

SLOW COOK Transfer the insert to the slow cooker, cover, and cook on the low-heat setting for 4 hours. The sauce should be thick and the flavors blended.

ASSEMBLE About 15 minutes before the sauce is ready, bring a large pot three-fourths full of water to a boil. Add 2 tablespoons salt and the pasta and cook until al dente, 2–4 minutes or according to the package directions. Drain the pasta and return to the pot.

When the sauce is ready, using a large spoon, skim off and discard as much fat as possible from the surface. Add the remaining 2 tablespoons butter and 1 teaspoon rosemary and stir until the butter melts. Add about ½ cup (4 fl oz/125 ml) of the sauce to the pasta and toss gently to coat.

SERVE Divide the pasta among shallow individual bowls and top with additional sauce. Sprinkle a little of the Parmesan over each serving and serve right away. Pass the remaining cheese at the table.

Lamb Stew
with
Irish Stout

Purists may insist on only using mutton, potatoes, onion, and water to make
a good Irish stew, but my version uses some modern luxuries, such as tender
leg of lamb, sweet carrots, dark stout, and beef broth for a full-flavored meal.
Serve it with a green salad and crusty bread to complete the meal.

ingredients

2 lb (1 kg) boneless lamb from the leg, cut
into 1½–2-inch (4–5-cm) pieces

Kosher salt and freshly ground pepper

2 tablespoons unsalted butter, if including
the optional browning step

2 tablespoons canola oil, if not including
the optional browning step

1 yellow onion, chopped

2 tablespoons all-purpose flour

1½ cups (12 fl oz/375 ml) low-sodium
beef broth

1 cup (8 fl oz/250 ml) stout or brown ale

4 Yukon gold potatoes, cut into large pieces

3 carrots, peeled and cut into large pieces

2 tablespoons chopped fresh
Italian parsley

makes 6–8 servings

step by step

PREP Season the lamb generously with salt and pepper.

BUILD FLAVOR (OPTIONAL) Put the slow-cooker insert on the stove
top over medium-high heat, then add the butter and warm until hot.
Add the lamb and cook, turning as needed, until browned on all sides,
about 10 minutes. Using a slotted spoon, transfer to a plate and set aside.

QUICK COOK If you have included the browning step, pour off all but
1 tablespoon of the fat from the insert and return the insert to medium-
high heat. If you are starting here, put the slow-cooker insert on the stove
top over medium-high heat, then add the oil and warm until hot. Add the
onion and cook, stirring, until the onions begin to soften, about 3 minutes.
Sprinkle the flour evenly over the onion and cook, stirring, until the flour
is fully incorporated, 1–2 minutes. Pour in the broth and stout and deglaze
the insert, stirring and scraping up the browned bits on the insert bottom
with a wooden spoon. Bring to a boil.

SLOW COOK Transfer the insert to the slow cooker, add the lamb, and
stir to coat evenly with the onion-broth mixture. Cover and cook on the
low-heat setting for 6 hours. The lamb should be tender.

Uncover and add the potatoes and carrots. Re-cover and continue to cook
on the low-heat setting for 2 hours. The potatoes should be fork-tender
and the lamb should be very tender.

ASSEMBLE Using a large spoon, skim off and discard as much fat as
possible from the surface of the cooking liquid. Transfer the lamb and
vegetables to a platter.

SERVE Spoon the cooking liquid over the top of the meat and vegetables,
sprinkle with the parsley, and serve right away.

Lamb Shanks
with
Tomatoes and Red Wine

Lamb shanks require low and slow cooking to become tender, but the resulting meaty flavor and velvety texture are more than worth the time. Serve them over creamy polenta or simmered white beans. For an easy topping, chop together equal parts fresh flat-leaf parsley and lemon zest to sprinkle over the shanks just before serving.

ingredients

½ cup (2½ oz/75 g) all-purpose flour

Kosher salt and freshly ground pepper

4 small lamb shanks, about 1 lb (500 g) each, trimmed of excess fat

2 tablespoons unsalted butter, if including the optional browning step

2 tablespoons canola oil

2 yellow onions, thinly sliced

1 carrot, peeled and chopped

1 rib celery, chopped

2 cloves garlic, minced

2 tomatoes, seeded and chopped

1 cup (8 fl oz/250 ml) dry red wine

1 cup (8 fl oz/250 ml) low-sodium beef broth

makes 4 servings

step by step

PREP On a plate, stir together the flour, 1 teaspoon salt, and ½ teaspoon pepper. Turn the shanks in the seasoned flour, coating evenly and shaking off any excess.

BUILD FLAVOR (OPTIONAL) Put the slow-cooker insert on the stove top over medium-high heat, then add the butter and oil and warm until hot. Add the lamb shanks and cook, turning as needed, until browned on all sides, about 10 minutes. Using tongs, transfer to a plate and set aside.

QUICK COOK If you have included the browning step, pour off all but 2 tablespoons of the fat from the insert and return the insert to medium-high heat. If you are starting here, put the slow-cooker insert on the stove top over medium-high heat, then add the oil and warm until hot. Add the onions, carrot, and celery and cook, stirring, until softened, about 5 minutes. Add the garlic and cook, stirring, for 1 minute. Stir in the tomatoes, wine, and broth and bring to a boil.

SLOW COOK Transfer the insert to the slow cooker, add the shanks, and spoon the broth mixture over the shanks to coat evenly. Cover and cook on the low-heat setting for 7—8 hours. The lamb should be very tender.

Uncover and continue to cook on the low-heat setting for about 1 hour to reduce the cooking liquid slightly.

ASSEMBLE Transfer the shanks to a plate and cover to keep warm. Using a large spoon, skim off and discard as much fat as possible from the surface of the cooking liquid. Strain the liquid through a fine-mesh sieve into a small saucepan, place over medium-high heat, and bring to a boil. Cook until reduced and slightly thickened, about 5 minutes.

SERVE Divide the shanks among individual plates and spoon the reduced cooking liquid over them. Serve right away.

Lamb Shanks
with
Olives and Herbs

This dish is inspired by the flavors of Provence, in southern France. If time permits, be sure to brown the lamb shanks, a step that enriches the flavor of this dinner party—worthy dish. Serve soft Parmesan polenta alongside.

ingredients

4 lb (2 kg) lamb shanks, in 4 equal pieces, each tied around the perimeter with kitchen string

Kosher salt and freshly ground pepper

2 tablespoons olive oil

2 carrots, peeled and finely chopped

2 ribs celery, finely chopped

1 red onion, finely chopped

1 teaspoon minced garlic

3 tablespoons all-purpose flour

2 tablespoons tomato paste

½ cup (4 fl oz/125 ml) hearty red wine

1–1½ cups (8–12 fl oz/250–375 ml) strained tomatoes

½ cup (4 fl oz/125 ml) fresh orange juice

½ cup (2½ oz/75 g) pitted black olives such as Kalamata

1 tablespoon mild honey

2 teaspoons herbes de Provence

Chopped fresh flat-leaf parsley for garnish (optional)

makes 4 servings

step by step

PREP Season the lamb shanks generously with salt and pepper.

BUILD FLAVOR (OPTIONAL) Put the slow-cooker insert on the stove top over medium-high heat, then add the oil and warm until hot. Add the lamb shanks and cook, turning as needed, until browned on all sides, about 10 minutes. Using tongs, transfer to a plate and set aside.

QUICK COOK If you have included the browning step, pour off all but 2 tablespoons of the fat from the insert and return the insert to medium-high heat. If you are starting here, put the slow-cooker insert on the stove top over medium-high heat, then add the oil and warm until hot. Add the carrots, celery, onion, and garlic and cook, stirring, until softened, 5 minutes. Whisk in the flour and tomato paste and cook, stirring, until the flour is fully incorporated, about 30 seconds. Pour in the wine and simmer until it evaporates, about 2 minutes. Add the tomatoes, orange juice, olives, honey, herbes de Provence, 1 teaspoon salt, and a few grinds of pepper, stir well, and bring to a boil.

SLOW COOK Transfer the insert to the slow cooker and add the lamb shanks, submerging them in the liquid. Cover and cook on the low-heat setting for 7 hours. The lamb should be very tender.

ASSEMBLE Transfer the lamb shanks to a platter and cover to keep warm. Using a large spoon, skim off and discard as much fat as possible from the cooking liquid.

SERVE Snip the strings on the lamb shanks, then transfer the shanks to individual plates. Spoon the cooking juices over the shanks, garnish with the parsley (if using), and serve right away.

Lamb Tagine
with
Dates and Almonds

The combination of dried fruits, toasted nuts, and fragrant spices typifies the tagines (stews) of North African kitchens. To save time, toast the almonds and halve the dates the night before you plan to serve the dish, then store in airtight containers. Serve this aromatic stew atop couscous sprinkled with chopped fresh parsley or cilantro.

ingredients

3 lb (1.5 kg) boneless lamb from the leg or shoulder, cut into 1½-inch (4-cm) cubes

Kosher salt and freshly ground black pepper

3 tablespoons olive oil

2 yellow onions, finely chopped

1 teaspoon ground cinnamon

1 teaspoon ground ginger

½ teaspoon ground cumin

¼ teaspoon cayenne pepper

¼ teaspoon saffron threads, crumbled

1½ cups (12 fl oz/375 ml) low-sodium chicken broth

1 cup (4½ oz/140 g) slivered almonds, toasted

1⅔ cups (10 oz/300 g) pitted dates, halved

2 tablespoons honey

makes 6—8 servings

step by step

PREP Season the lamb with 1 teaspoon each salt and black pepper.

BUILD FLAVOR (OPTIONAL) Put the slow-cooker insert on the stove top over medium-high heat, then add the oil and warm until hot. Working in batches if necessary to avoid crowding, add the lamb and cook, turning as needed, until browned on all sides, about 10 minutes. Using a slotted spoon, transfer to a plate and set aside.

QUICK COOK If you have included the browning step, pour off all but 3 tablespoons of the fat from the insert and return the insert to medium-high heat. If you are starting here, put the slow-cooker insert on the stove top over medium-high heat, then add the oil and warm until hot. Add the onions and cook, stirring, until just starting to brown, 5—7 minutes. Add the cinnamon, ginger, cumin, cayenne, and saffron and cook, stirring, until the spices are fragrant and evenly coat the onions, about 1 minute. Pour in the broth and deglaze the insert, stirring and scraping up the browned bits on the insert bottom with a wooden spoon. Bring to a boil.

SLOW COOK Transfer the insert to the slow cooker, add the lamb, and stir to coat evenly with the broth mixture. Cover and cook on the low-heat setting for 8 hours. The lamb should be very tender.

ASSEMBLE Uncover the slow cooker and, using a large spoon, skim off and discard as much fat as possible from the cooking liquid. Add the almonds and dates. Drizzle in the honey and stir to combine, making sure that the dates are submerged in the cooking liquid. Re-cover and cook on the low-heat setting for about 10 minutes to soften the dates. Taste and adjust the seasoning with salt and pepper.

SERVE Spoon the tagine onto individual plates or a platter and serve right away.

Spicy Lamb Curry
with
Spinach and Yogurt

A bit spicy, and loaded with flavor, this fragrant Indian curry is almost a
one-dish meal. All you need to round out the menu is some basmati rice to soak up
the sauce. You can adjust the amount of heat by increasing or decreasing the
amount of jalapeños in the dish. For a really fiery curry, leave in the chile seeds.

ingredients

3 lb (1.5 kg) boneless lamb from the leg,
cut into 1½-inch (4-cm) cubes

Kosher salt and freshly ground pepper

½ cup (4 fl oz/125 ml) canola oil

2 yellow onions, finely chopped

4 cloves garlic, minced

3 small jalapeño chiles, seeded and minced

1-inch (2.5-cm) piece fresh ginger,
peeled and grated

1 tablespoon brown mustard seeds

1 tablespoon ground cumin

1 tablespoon ground coriander

1½ teaspoons ground cardamom

1 teaspoon ground turmeric

1½ cups (12 fl oz/375 ml) low-sodium
chicken broth

10 oz (315 g) baby spinach

1 tablespoon garam masala

1 cup (8 oz/250 g) plain yogurt

makes 6—8 servings

step by step

PREP Season the lamb with 1 teaspoon salt and ½ teaspoon pepper.

BUILD FLAVOR (OPTIONAL) Put the slow-cooker insert on the stove top
over medium-high heat, then add the oil and warm until hot. Working in
batches if necessary to avoid crowding, add the lamb and cook, turning
as needed, until browned on all sides, about 10 minutes. Using a slotted
spoon, transfer to a plate and set aside.

QUICK COOK If you have included the browning step, pour off all but
½ cup (4 fl oz/125 ml) of the fat from the insert and return the insert to
medium-high heat. If you are starting here, put the slow-cooker insert
on the stove top over medium-high heat, then add the oil and warm until
hot. Add the onions and cook, stirring, until golden brown, 7—10 minutes.
Add the garlic, chiles, ginger, mustard, cumin, coriander, cardamom, and
turmeric and stir until the spices are fragrant and evenly coat the onions,
about 1 minute. Pour in the broth and deglaze the insert, stirring and
scraping up the browned bits on the insert bottom with a wooden spoon.
Bring to a boil.

SLOW COOK Transfer the insert to the slow cooker, add the lamb, and
stir to coat evenly with the broth mixture. Cover and cook on the low-heat
setting for 8 hours. The lamb should be very tender.

ASSEMBLE Add the spinach, re-cover, and cook for 15 minutes. Uncover,
sprinkle evenly with the garam masala, and stir to combine.

SERVE Spoon the curry into shallow individual bowls, garnish with the
yogurt, and serve right away.

Lamb Meatballs
with
Golden Raisins and Capers

Once you have prepped and shaped the meatballs, which goes very quickly (and can be done the night before you plan to cook), this recipe is a breeze. The meatballs cook relatively quickly too, in just 4 hours, in a Sicilian-inspired sauce accented with sweet-and-sour flavors. Accompany with a green salad with orange vinaigrette.

ingredients

1½ lb (750 g) ground lamb

1 cup (4 oz/125 g) dried bread crumbs

1 cup (4 oz/125 g) freshly grated pecorino cheese

1 large egg, lightly beaten

2 teaspoons minced fresh rosemary

Kosher salt and freshly ground pepper

4 cups (32 fl oz/1 l) strained tomatoes

¼ cup (1½ oz/45 g) golden raisins

¼ cup (2 fl oz/60 ml) balsamic vinegar

3 tablespoons tomato paste

3 tablespoons capers, rinsed

1 tablespoon olive oil

2 teaspoons minced garlic

1 lb (500 g) spaghetti

¼ cup (1¼ oz/35 g) pine nuts, toasted

makes 4—6 servings

step by step

PREP In a large bowl, combine the lamb, bread crumbs, cheese, egg, rosemary, ½ teaspoon salt, and a few grinds of pepper and gently knead together with your hands to distribute the ingredients evenly. Shape into 20 balls, each 1-inch (2.5 cm) in diameter.

SLOW COOK In the slow cooker, stir together the tomatoes, raisins, vinegar, tomato paste, capers, oil, garlic, and ½ teaspoon salt, mixing well. Add the meatballs, submerging them in the sauce. Cover and cook on the low-heat setting for 4 hours. The meatballs should be cooked through in the center.

ASSEMBLE About 15 minutes before the meatballs and sauce are ready, bring a large pot three-fourths full of water to a boil. Add 2 tablespoons salt and the pasta and cook until al dente, according to the package directions. Drain the pasta and return to the pot. Add ½ cup (4 fl oz/125 ml) of the sauce and toss gently to coat.

SERVE Divide the pasta among shallow individual bowls and top with the meatballs and the remaining sauce. Garnish each serving with the pine nuts and serve right away.

Pork

Pork Ramen

The finest Japanese pork ramen takes considerable culinary skill and many hours to create. Here is a simplified, yet still delicious, version that boasts plenty of succulent braised pork. If you can't find high-quality fresh ramen noodles, use fresh thin Chinese egg noodles or fresh linguine. Serve the soup with your favorite ramen embellishments. I like to top my bowl with a soft-boiled egg and some baby spinach.

ingredients

3 lb (1.5 kg) boneless pork shoulder, cut into 3 equal pieces

Kosher salt

2 tablespoons canola oil, if including the optional browning step

1 yellow onion, coarsely chopped

6 cloves garlic, chopped

2-inch (5-cm) piece fresh ginger, peeled and chopped

8 cups (64 fl oz/2 l) low-sodium chicken broth

1 leek, white and green parts, halved lengthwise and coarsely chopped

¼ lb (125 g) cremini or button mushrooms, brushed clean and coarsely chopped

Low-sodium soy sauce for seasoning

Sesame and/or chile oil for seasoning

1½ lb (750 g) fresh ramen noodles

8 large eggs (optional)

About 4 green onions, white and pale green parts, finely chopped

makes 8 servings

step by step

PREP Season the pork with salt.

BUILD FLAVOR (OPTIONAL) Put the slow-cooker insert on the stove top over medium-high heat, then add the oil and warm until hot. Working in batches if necessary to avoid crowding, add the pork pieces and sear them on the first side without moving them until well browned, 3–4 minutes. Turn the pieces and sear on the second side until well browned, 3–4 minutes longer. Transfer to a plate and set aside.

Pour off all but 2 tablespoons of the fat from the insert and return the insert to medium-high heat. Add the yellow onion and sear, without stirring, until browned, about 5 minutes. Stir in the garlic, ginger, and 1 cup (8 fl oz/250 ml) of the broth and deglaze the insert, stirring and scraping up any browned bits from the insert bottom, then let simmer for 1 minute.

SLOW COOK If you have included the browning step, transfer the insert to the slow cooker, add the leek, mushrooms, and the remaining 7 cups (56 fl oz/1.75 l) broth, and stir to combine. If you are starting here, combine the pork, yellow onion, garlic, ginger, leek, mushrooms, and broth in the slow cooker. Cover and cook on the low-heat setting for 8 hours. The pork should be very tender and the broth should be fragrant.

ASSEMBLE Transfer the pork to a cutting board. Using 2 forks, break the pork into bite-size chunks, removing and discarding any large pieces of fat. Strain the broth through a fine-mesh sieve into a bowl and discard the solids. Using a large spoon, skim off and discard any fat from the surface of the broth. Return the pork and broth to the slow cooker and season to taste with soy sauce and sesame and/or chile oil. Cover and cook on the low heat setting for about 30 minutes to warm through.

Cook the ramen noodles according to the package directions. If you want to top each bowl of ramen with an egg, put the eggs into boiling water and simmer for 5–6 minutes. Remove the eggs from the water, let cool until they can be handled, and peel them.

SERVE Divide the noodles evenly among individual bowls. Ladle the broth and pork over the noodles, dividing them evenly, then sprinkle with the green onions. If desired, top each bowl with a halved soft-boiled egg and serve right away.

Chile Verde

Literally "green chile," this popular Mexican-influenced stew is on the menu at many a taqueria and it could not be simpler to make. Bite-size chunks of tender pork are combined with mild green chiles and tangy tomatillos. Serve it with hot steamed rice and sliced avocados with a squirt of lime juice, or stuff it into warm tortillas for tacos.

ingredients

4 lb (2 kg) boneless pork shoulder, trimmed of excess fat and cut into 1-inch (2.5-cm) cubes

Kosher salt and freshly ground pepper

4 cans (7 oz/220 g each) diced fire-roasted mild green chiles, drained

2 cans (12 oz/375 g each) whole tomatillos, drained and broken up by hand

1 large yellow onion, finely chopped

4 cloves garlic, minced

1 large jalapeño chile, seeded and minced

2 cups (16 fl oz/500 ml) low-sodium chicken broth

¾ lb (375 g) firm, ripe tomatoes, finely chopped

1 tablespoon dried oregano

2 teaspoons ground cumin

Sour cream and chopped fresh cilantro for serving

makes 8–10 servings

step by step

PREP Season the pork with 2 teaspoons salt and 1 teaspoon pepper.

SLOW COOK In the slow cooker, combine the pork, mild chiles, tomatillos, onion, garlic, jalapeño chile, broth, tomatoes, oregano, and cumin and stir to mix well. Cover and cook on the low-heat setting for 8 hours. The pork should be very tender and a thick sauce will have formed in the bottom of the slow cooker.

SERVE Ladle the chile into individual bowls, top with a little sour cream and cilantro, and serve right away.

Pulled Pork

This crowd-pleasing recipe is great for a big family get-together. You can keep the pork warm in the slow cooker on low and set it out on a buffet along with a basket of soft buns. Pick up some coleslaw, baked beans, and potato salad from the deli, set out bottles of cold beer or sparkling lemonade, and your work is done. Be sure to choose a good-quality barbecue sauce that is more vinegary than it is sweet.

ingredients

1 boneless pork shoulder, about 3 lb (1.5 kg), tied with string by the butcher

Kosher salt and freshly ground pepper

2 tablespoons canola oil

1 yellow onion, chopped

1 clove garlic, minced

½ cup (4 fl oz/125 ml) low-sodium chicken broth

2 cups (16 fl oz/500 ml) good-quality bottled barbecue sauce, plus more for serving

3 tablespoons yellow mustard

¼ cup (3 oz/90 g) honey (optional)

makes 4 servings

step by step

PREP Season the pork generously with salt and pepper.

BUILD FLAVOR (OPTIONAL) Put the slow-cooker insert on the stove top over medium-high heat, then add the oil and warm until hot. Add the pork and cook, turning frequently, until browned on all sides, about 10 minutes. Transfer to a plate and set aside.

QUICK COOK If you have included the browning step, pour off all but 2 tablespoons of the fat from the insert and return the insert to medium-high heat. If you are starting here, put the slow-cooker insert on the stove top over medium-high heat, then add the oil and warm until hot. Add the onion and cook, stirring, until softened, about 5 minutes. Add the garlic and cook, stirring, for 1 minute. Pour in the broth and season with salt and pepper.

SLOW COOK Transfer the insert to the slow cooker and add the pork. Cover and cook on the low-heat setting for 8–10 hours. The pork should be very tender.

ASSEMBLE Transfer the pork to a platter and let cool slightly. Cut away the strings. Using 2 forks, pull the pork into shreds, removing and discarding any large pieces of fat and gristle.

Return the shredded pork to the cooker. Add the barbecue sauce, mustard, and honey, if using, season with salt and pepper, and stir to mix well. Cook uncovered on the high-heat setting, stirring frequently, until the flavors are well blended and the sauce has thickened, about 30 minutes.

SERVE Spoon the pork and its sauce into a warm serving bowl and serve right away. Pass additional barbecue sauce at the table.

Carnitas

Mexican carnitas are traditionally made by slowly simmering large chunks
of pork shoulder in the pork's own fat, rendering it incredibly tender. In this
version I use citrus juice and a small amount of olive oil for a healthier preparation.
Set out warm corn tortillas, lime wedges, pickled onion, chopped fresh cilantro,
and crumbled queso fresco and let diners assemble their own tacos.

ingredients

1 boneless pork shoulder, 3–4 lb (1.5–2 kg)

Kosher salt and freshly ground pepper

1–2 tablespoons olive oil

1 yellow onion, finely chopped

2 cloves garlic, minced

1½ cups (12 fl oz/375 ml) Mexican
lager-style beer

Grated zest and juice of 1 large orange

Grated zest and juice of 1 lime

1 tablespoon dried oregano

makes 6–8 servings

step by step

PREP Season the pork with 2 teaspoons salt and 1 teaspoon pepper.

BUILD FLAVOR (OPTIONAL) Put the slow-cooker insert on the stove
top over medium-high heat, then add 2 tablespoons oil and warm until
hot. Add the pork and cook, turning frequently, until browned on all sides,
about 10 minutes. Transfer to a plate and set aside.

QUICK COOK If you have included the browning step, pour off all but
1 tablespoon of the fat from the insert. If you are starting here, put the
slow-cooker insert on the stove top over medium-high heat, then add
1 tablespoon oil and warm until hot. Add the onion and garlic and cook,
stirring, until they begin to soften, 1–2 minutes. Pour in the beer and
deglaze the insert, scraping up the browned bits on the insert bottom
with a wooden spoon. Bring to a boil.

SLOW COOK Transfer the insert to the slow cooker and add the pork.
Add the orange and lime zests and juices and the oregano, distributing
them evenly. Cover and cook on the low-heat setting for 10 hours. The
pork should be very tender.

ASSEMBLE Transfer the pork to a cutting board and tent with aluminum
foil to keep warm. Using a large spoon, skim off and discard as much fat
as possible from the surface of the cooking liquid. Using 2 forks, coarsely
shred the pork into bite-size pieces, discarding any large pieces of fat.

SERVE Arrange the pork on a platter, moisten it lightly with the cooking
juices, and serve right away.

Vietnamese Pork Chops
with
Garlic and Lemongrass

This simple slow-cooked version of a grilled Vietnamese classic is packed with the heady flavors of lemongrass, garlic, and soy sauce. Accompany the chops with sticky rice and seared bok choy for a meal worthy of company.

ingredients

¼ cup (2 oz/60 g) firmly packed golden brown sugar

6 cloves garlic, minced

2 large shallots, finely chopped

2 stalks lemongrass, tender bulb part only, trimmed, tough outer layers discarded, and minced

3 tablespoons low-sodium soy sauce

3 tablespoons Asian fish sauce

Freshly ground pepper

4–6 bone-in center-cut pork chops, each about 1 inch (2.5 cm) thick and 6–8 oz (185–250 g)

1 cup (8 fl oz/250 ml) low-sodium chicken or beef broth

makes 4–6 servings

step by step

PREP To make a marinade, in a bowl, stir together the sugar, garlic, shallots, lemongrass, soy sauce, fish sauce, and ½ teaspoon pepper; the marinade will be fairly dry. Place the pork chops in a large zippered plastic bag, add the marinade, and seal the bag closed. Turn the bag over a few times to coat the pork chops evenly with the marinade, then refrigerate overnight.

SLOW COOK The next day, transfer the chops and their marinade to the slow cooker. Pour in the broth, cover, and cook on the low-heat setting for 6 hours. The chops should be very tender.

ASSEMBLE Transfer the pork chops to a platter. Using a large spoon, skim off and discard as much fat as possible from the surface of the cooking liquid. Strain the liquid through a fine-mesh sieve into a small bowl and set aside.

SERVE Divide the chops evenly among individual plates and drizzle some of the cooking liquid over each chop. Serve right away.

Pork Chops Smothered
with
Savory Onion Sauce

Browning the meat and thickening the sauce for this classic southern dish take a little extra time—about 15 minutes—but the delicious results merit the two additional steps. Serve the pork chops over steamed rice and topped with plenty of sauce.

ingredients

6 thick-cut bone-in center-cut pork chops, each about 1½ inches (4 cm) thick and ¾ lb (375 g)

Kosher salt and freshly ground pepper

4 slices thick-cut bacon

Olive oil, if needed

3 tablespoons all-purpose flour

2 cups (16 fl oz/500 ml) low-sodium chicken broth

2 tablespoons Worcestershire sauce

1 tablespoon cider vinegar

1 tablespoon firmly packed dark brown sugar

2 yellow onions, finely chopped

2 ribs celery, finely chopped

2 cloves garlic, minced

1 sprig fresh thyme

2 bay leaves

makes 6–8 servings

step by step

PREP Season the pork chops generously with salt.

BUILD FLAVOR Put the slow-cooker insert on the stove top over medium heat. Add the bacon and fry, turning occasionally, until crisp, about 5 minutes. Transfer the bacon to paper towels to drain.

Raise the heat to medium-high and add half of the pork chops. Cook, turning once, until browned on both sides, about 6 minutes total. Transfer to a plate and repeat with the remaining chops, adding them to the plate.

QUICK COOK Check the amount of fat in the insert. If you have less than 2 tablespoons, add oil as needed to total that amount. If you have more than 2 tablespoons, pour off the excess, then return the insert to medium heat. Whisk the flour into the fat, then slowly pour in the broth while whisking constantly and scraping up the browned bits on the insert bottom. Continue to whisk until the mixture is smooth, then stir in the Worcestershire sauce, vinegar, sugar, onions, celery, garlic, thyme, and bay leaves until combined.

SLOW COOK Transfer the insert to the slow cooker and add the pork chops, layering them as needed to make them fit. Cover and cook on the low-heat setting for 6 hours. The pork chops should be very tender.

SERVE Transfer the chops to a platter, top with the sauce, and serve right away.

Pork Chops
with
Garlic, Soy, and Sriracha

You can use this same sauce to flavor bone-in chicken thighs or cubed beef chuck with equally delicious results. These lean chops can dry out if cooked too long, so check them after just 2 hours in the slow cooker. Accompany with steamed rice and wilted greens.

ingredients

6 bone-in pork loin chops, each 1 inch (2.5 cm) thick and ¾ lb (375 g)

Kosher salt and freshly ground pepper

1 tablespoon peanut oil

1 yellow onion, finely chopped

1 tablespoon minced garlic

1 tablespoon peeled and minced fresh ginger

3 tablespoons all-purpose flour

1 cup (8 fl oz/250 ml) low-sodium chicken broth

½ cup (4 fl oz/125 ml) low-sodium soy sauce

½ cup (4 fl oz/125 ml) rice vinegar

¼ cup plus 1 tablespoon (2½ oz/75 g) firmly packed dark brown sugar

1 tablespoon Sriracha sauce, or more to taste

Sliced green onions, white and pale green parts, for garnish

makes 6 servings

step by step

PREP Season the chops generously with salt and pepper.

QUICK COOK Place the slow-cooker insert on the stove top over medium-high heat, then add the oil and warm until hot. Add the yellow onion, garlic, and ginger and cook, stirring, until softened, about 5 minutes. Whisk in the flour and cook, stirring, until the flour is fully incorporated, about 30 seconds. Add the broth, soy sauce, vinegar, sugar, and Sriracha sauce, stir well, and bring to a boil.

SLOW COOK Transfer the insert to the slow cooker and add the pork chops, submerging them in the sauce. Cover and cook on the low-heat setting for 2–3 hours. The meat should be tender and still succulent.

SERVE Divide the chops among individual plates and spoon the sauce over the top. Sprinkle with the green onions and serve right away.

Pork and Ricotta Meatballs
with
Garlicky Tomato Sauce

Ricotta cheese and fresh bread crumbs help keep these meatballs succulent.
You can make the bread crumbs in advance and store them in a zippered
plastic bag in the freezer for up to 3 months. Serve the meatballs and sauce
tucked into hoagie rolls or spooned on top of pasta or sautéed spinach.

ingredients

3 lb (1.5 kg) ground pork

½ lb (250 g) good-quality sliced
white bread, processed into
crumbs in a food processor

1 large yellow onion, minced

1 cup (8 oz/250 g) ricotta cheese

4 large eggs, lightly beaten

1 teaspoon ground fennel

Kosher salt and freshly ground pepper

2 cans (28 oz/875 g each) crushed
tomatoes, with juice

1 can (15 oz/470 g) tomato sauce

1 teaspoon fresh oregano leaves

3 cloves garlic, minced

1 large sprig fresh basil, plus chopped
basil for garnish (optional)

Freshly grated Parmesan cheese
for garnish

makes 8–10 servings

step by step

PREP To make the meatballs, in a large bowl, combine the pork, bread crumbs, half of the onion, the ricotta, the eggs, the fennel, 1 teaspoon salt, and a few grinds of pepper. Using a wooden spoon, mix well.

Oil 2 large rimmed baking sheets. To shape each meatball, scoop up about 3½ tablespoons of the meat mixture and roll between your palms. As the balls are ready, arrange them on the prepared baking sheets, dividing them evenly between the pans and spacing them at least 1 inch (2.5 cm) apart. You should have 30–34 meatballs. Cover and refrigerate for up to 24 hours.

SLOW COOK (PART ONE) To make the sauce, in the slow cooker, combine the tomatoes, tomato sauce, the remaining onion, the oregano, garlic, basil sprig (if using), 1 teaspoon salt, and a few grinds of pepper and stir well. Cover and cook on the low-heat setting for 1 hour.

QUICK COOK About 30 minutes before the sauce is ready, position 2 oven racks in the middle of the oven and preheat the oven to 450°F (230°C). Roast the meatballs, rotating the pans between the racks and from front to back about halfway through the cooking, until browned, about 20 minutes. Using a slotted spoon, transfer the meatballs to the sauce. Discard any fat on the pans.

SLOW COOK (PART TWO) Cover and cook on the low-heat setting for 4 hours. The meatballs should be cooked through and the sauce should be flavorful. Remove and discard the basil.

SERVE Using a slotted spoon, transfer the meatballs to a platter and spoon the sauce over the top. Garnish with the chopped basil, if using, and the cheese and serve right away.

Sweet-and-Sour Pork

This crowd-pleasing blend of tender pork shoulder, juicy pineapple, and sweet red peppers simmered in a spicy-tangy-sweet sauce is nothing like the fluorescent deep-fried dish found under the same name in some restaurants. Accompany with steamed rice and a quick sauté of greens and garlic.

ingredients

4½ lb (2.25 kg) boneless pork shoulder, cut into 3 or 4 equal pieces

Kosher salt

1 large can (20 oz/625 g) plus 1 small can (8 oz/250 g) pineapple chunks in juice

¼ cup (2 fl oz/60 ml) rice vinegar

2 tablespoons cornstarch dissolved in ¼ cup (2 fl oz/60 ml) water

2 tablespoons low-sodium soy sauce

¼ cup (2 oz/60 g) firmly packed golden brown sugar

2 tablespoons canola oil, if including the optional browning step

1 red bell pepper, seeded and cut lengthwise into strips

1 yellow onion, halved and thinly sliced

2 fresh red chiles such as Fresno or serrano, seeded and chopped

3 cloves garlic, minced

makes 6—8 servings

step by step

PREP Season the pork with salt. Drain both cans of pineapple, reserving the fruit and juice separately. Cover the pineapple chunks and refrigerate until needed. Measure 1 cup (8 fl oz/250 ml) of the juice and pour into a bowl. Discard the remaining juice or reserve for another use. Add the vinegar, cornstarch mixture, soy sauce, and sugar to the pineapple juice and whisk to combine.

BUILD FLAVOR (OPTIONAL) Put the slow-cooker insert on the stove top over medium-high heat, then add the oil and warm until hot. Working in batches to avoid crowding, add the pork pieces and sear them on the first side without moving them until well browned, 3—4 minutes. Turn the pieces and sear on the second side until well browned, 3—4 minutes longer. Transfer to a plate and repeat with the remaining pieces, adding them to the plate.

SLOW COOK If you have included the browning step, pour off the fat from the insert and transfer the insert to the slow cooker. Add the browned pork, bell pepper, onion, chiles, and garlic and toss and stir as needed to combine the vegetables evenly with the pork. If you are starting here, combine the pork and vegetables in the slow cooker and toss and stir as directed to mix evenly. Briefly whisk the pineapple juice mixture, then pour evenly over the pork and vegetables. Cover and cook on the low-heat setting for 6 hours.

Uncover, add the reserved pineapple chunks, and stir to mix evenly. Re-cover and continue to cook on the low-heat setting for 2 hours longer. The pork should be very tender.

ASSEMBLE Transfer the pork to a cutting board. Using 2 forks, break the pork into bite-size chunks, discarding any large pieces of fat. Transfer the pork to a bowl and cover to keep warm. Using a large spoon, skim off and discard any fat from the surface of the cooking liquid. If you like, strain the cooking liquid through a fine-mesh sieve into a saucepan and add the pineapple and vegetables to the bowl holding the pork. Put the pan over medium-high heat, bring to a boil, and boil until the liquid is syrupy, 5—10 minutes.

SERVE Transfer the pork, pineapple, and vegetables to a platter and pour the cooking liquid over the top. Serve right away.

Honey-Ginger Pork
with
Braised Kale

My family can never get enough of this dish, with its sweet, salty, bitter, spicy flavors.
If you like lots of greens, you can add a second bunch of kale, but you will need
to stir it three or four times as it cooks. Serve over soba (buckwheat) noodles
or other Asian noodles and top with a sprinkle of toasted sesame seeds.

ingredients

4–4½ lb (2–2.25 kg) boneless pork
shoulder, cut into 3 equal pieces

Kosher salt

⅓ cup (3 fl oz/80 ml) mirin or
medium-dry white wine

¼ cup (2 fl oz/60 ml) tamari or
low-sodium soy sauce

3 tablespoons honey, warmed

4 large cloves garlic, minced

1 heaping tablespoon peeled and grated
fresh ginger

½ yellow onion, chopped

1 jalapeño chile, sliced (optional)

2 tablespoons canola oil, if including
the optional browning step

1 large bunch kale, preferably lacinato
kale, ribs removed and leaves chopped

makes 6–8 servings

step by step

PREP Season the pork pieces with salt. In a small bowl, stir together
mirin, soy sauce, honey, garlic, ginger, onion, and the chile, if using.

BUILD FLAVOR (OPTIONAL) Put the slow-cooker insert on the stove
top over medium-high heat, then add the oil and warm until hot. Working
in batches if necessary to avoid crowding, add the pork pieces and
sear them on the first side, without moving them, until well browned,
3–4 minutes. Turn the pieces and sear on the second side until well
browned, 3–4 minutes longer.

SLOW COOK Transfer the insert to the slow cooker and pour the mirin-
soy mixture over the pork. If you have skipped the browning step, put
the pork in the slow cooker and pour in the mirin-soy mixture. Toss to
coat the pork evenly with the mixture. Cover and cook on the low-heat
setting for 8 hours. About 1 hour before the pork is ready, stir in the kale.
The pork should be very tender and the kale should be tender.

ASSEMBLE Transfer the pork to a cutting board. Break the pork into
large chunks, discarding any large pieces of fat. Using a large spoon,
skim off and discard any fat from the surface of the cooking liquid.
Return the meat to the slow cooker and stir gently to combine.

SERVE Spoon the pork, kale, and cooking liquid onto a platter or
individual plates. Serve right away.

Stuffed Pork Loin
with
Dried Apricots

Just about any kind of fruit is a classic complement for pork. Here, dried apricots paired with orange juice, mustard, and fresh thyme create a sweet-sour accent for lean pork loin. Serve with mashed potatoes and a green salad for a complete meal.

ingredients

¼ cup (1½ oz/45 g) all-purpose flour

Kosher salt and freshly ground pepper

1 boneless pork loin roast, about 2½ lb (1.25 kg)

2 tablespoons canola oil

1 yellow onion, thinly sliced

1 clove garlic, minced

1 cup (8 fl oz/250 ml) low-sodium chicken broth

3 cups (18 oz/560 g) dried apricots

½ cup (4 fl oz/125 ml) fresh orange juice

2 tablespoons chopped fresh thyme

2 tablespoons Dijon mustard

makes 4–6 servings

step by step

PREP On a plate, stir together the flour, ½ teaspoon salt, and ¼ teaspoon pepper. Turn the pork roast in the seasoned flour, coating evenly and shaking off any excess.

BUILD FLAVOR (OPTIONAL) Put the slow-cooker insert on the stove top over medium-high heat, then add the oil and warm until hot. Add the pork and cook, turning frequently, until browned on all sides, 5–8 minutes. Transfer to a plate and set aside.

QUICK COOK If you have included the browning step, pour off all but 1 tablespoon of the fat from the insert. If you are starting here, put the slow-cooker insert on the stove top over medium-high heat, then add the oil and warm until hot. Add the onion and cook, stirring, until softened, 3–5 minutes. Add the garlic and cook, stirring, for 1 minute. Pour in the broth and deglaze the pan, stirring and scraping up the browned bits on the insert bottom with a wooden spoon. Bring to a boil.

SLOW COOK Transfer the insert to the slow cooker and add the pork. Then add the apricots, orange juice, and thyme, distributing them evenly. Cover and cook on the low-heat setting for 4–6 hours. The pork is ready when an instant-read thermometer inserted into the center reads 140°F (60°C).

ASSEMBLE Transfer the pork to a cutting board and tent with aluminum foil to keep warm. Using a slotted spoon, transfer the apricots to a bowl and set aside. Using a large spoon, skim off and discard as much fat as possible from the surface of the cooking liquid. Strain the juices through a fine-mesh sieve into a saucepan. Place over high heat, bring to a boil, and cook, stirring occasionally, until reduced and the flavors are concentrated, about 10 minutes. Whisk the mustard into the sauce, add the apricots, and stir to mix well. Season with salt and pepper. Transfer the sauce to a bowl. Using a large, sharp knife, cut the pork across the grain into thin slices.

SERVE Arrange the pork slices on a platter and serve right away. Pass the sauce at the table.

Pork Shoulder
with
Sauerkraut and Apples

In this German-influenced recipe, the tangy flavor of sauerkraut and the sweetness of apples complement the richness of slow-simmered pork. The prep is minimal and the cooking time is long and unattended, perfect for a busy day. Serve with roasted potatoes.

ingredients

1 boneless pork shoulder roast, 4–5 lb (2–2.5 kg), tied with string by the butcher

Kosher salt and freshly ground pepper

2 tablespoons unsalted butter, if including the optional browning step

2 tablespoons canola oil

1 yellow onion, thinly sliced

3 Golden Delicious apples, peeled, halved, cored, and cut into wedges

1 tablespoon fresh thyme leaves

½ cup (4 fl oz/125 ml) dry white wine

2 lb (1 kg) sauerkraut, squeezed dry

¼ cup (2 oz/60 g) firmly packed dark brown sugar

1 tablespoon caraway seeds

makes 4–6 servings

step by step

PREP Season the pork generously with salt and pepper.

BUILD FLAVOR (OPTIONAL) Put the slow-cooker insert on the stove top over medium-high heat, then add the butter and oil and warm until hot. Add the pork and cook, turning frequently, until browned on all sides, about 10 minutes. Transfer to a plate and set aside.

QUICK COOK If you have included the browning step, pour off all but 2 tablespoons of the fat from the insert and return the insert to medium-high heat. If you are starting here, put the slow-cooker insert on the stove top over medium-high heat, then add the oil and warm until hot. Add the onion, apples, and thyme and sauté until the onion and apples are lightly browned, 8–10 minutes. Transfer to a bowl and set aside.

Pour off the fat from the insert and return the insert to medium-high heat. Add the wine and deglaze the insert, stirring and scraping up the browned bits on the insert bottom with a wooden spoon. Pour the wine mixture into a bowl and set aside. Cover the bottom of the insert with the sauerkraut, then sprinkle it evenly with the sugar and caraway seeds. Place the pork on top and surround with the apple mixture. Pour in the wine mixture.

SLOW COOK Transfer the insert to the slow cooker, cover, and cook on the low-heat setting for 8 hours. The pork should be fork-tender.

ASSEMBLE Transfer the pork to a cutting board, tent with aluminum foil, and let rest for 10 minutes. Using a large, sharp knife, cut the pork across the grain into slices about ½ inch (12 mm) thick, removing the strings as you slice.

SERVE Spoon the sauerkraut, apples, and cooking juices onto a large platter. Top with the pork slices and serve right away.

Pork and Squash Stew
with
Bourbon and Sage

Perfumed with sweet bourbon and earthy sage, this combination of pork and hard-shelled squash is an ideal autumn dish. If you like a bit of heat, add a sliced serrano chile along with the onion. Complete the menu with a salad of greens and red onion.

ingredients

3–4 lb (1.5–2 kg) boneless pork shoulder, cut into 3 equal pieces

Kosher salt and freshly ground pepper

2 tablespoons canola oil, if including the optional browning step

1 large yellow onion, quartered and thinly sliced

2 tablespoons finely chopped fresh sage

1½ cups (12 fl oz/375 ml) low-sodium chicken broth

⅓ cup (3 fl oz/80 ml) sweet bourbon

3 cups (14 oz/440 g) cubed butternut squash

makes 6 servings

step by step

PREP Season the pork with salt and pepper.

BUILD FLAVOR (OPTIONAL) Put the slow-cooker insert on the stove top over medium-high heat, then add the oil and warm until hot. Working in batches if necessary to avoid crowding, add the pork pieces and sear them on the first side without moving them until well browned, 3–4 minutes. Turn the pieces and sear on the second side until well browned, 3–4 minutes longer.

SLOW COOK Transfer the insert to the slow cooker, add the onion, sage, broth, and bourbon, and stir to mix well. If you have skipped the browning step, put the pork in the slow cooker, add the onion, sage, broth, and bourbon, and stir to mix well. Cover and cook on the low-heat setting for 6 hours.

Uncover and use a large spoon to skim off and discard as much fat as possible from the surface of the cooking liquid. Add the squash, submerging it in the liquid and distributing it evenly around the pork. Re-cover and continue to cook on the low-heat setting for 2 hours longer. The squash should be tender and the pork should fall apart when tested with a fork.

ASSEMBLE Using a large spoon, skim off and discard as much fat as possible from the surface of the cooking liquid. Transfer the pork to a cutting board. Using 2 forks, break the pork into large chunks, discarding any large pieces of fat. Return the meat to the slow cooker and stir gently to combine.

SERVE Transfer the pork, squash, and cooking liquid to a serving bowl or platter and serve right away.

Beer-Braised Pork Roast

Either pork butt (the upper part of the shoulder) or pork shoulder (the lower part of the shoulder) can be used in this recipe. Serve it with steamed broccoli tossed with butter and grated lemon zest and hunks of sourdough bread.

ingredients

1 boneless pork butt or pork shoulder roast, about 4 lb (2 kg), trimmed

Kosher salt and freshly ground pepper

2 tablespoons canola oil

2 yellow onions, thinly sliced

1 carrot, peeled and chopped

2 cloves garlic, minced

1 tablespoon tomato paste

3 tablespoons all-purpose flour

1 bottle (12 fl oz/375 ml) dark beer

½ cup (4 fl oz/125 ml) apple cider

1 cup (8 fl oz/250 ml) low-sodium chicken broth

1 tablespoon cider vinegar

5–6 sprigs fresh thyme

makes 4–6 servings

step by step

PREP Season the pork generously with salt and pepper.

BUILD FLAVOR (OPTIONAL) Put the slow-cooker insert on the stove top over medium-high heat, then add the oil and warm until hot. Add the pork and cook, turning frequently, until browned on all sides, about 10 minutes. Transfer to a plate and set aside.

QUICK COOK If you have included the browning step, pour off all but 1 tablespoon of the fat from the insert. If you are starting here, put the slow-cooker insert on the stove top over medium-high heat, then add the oil and warm until hot. Add the onions and carrot and cook, stirring, until softened, about 5 minutes. Add the garlic and cook, stirring, for 1 minute. Stir in the tomato paste and cook, stirring, until the mixture starts to become dry, about 2 minutes. Add the flour and cook, stirring constantly to prevent scorching, for 2 minutes. Pour in the beer and deglaze the insert, stirring and scraping up the browned bits on the insert bottom with a wooden spoon. Cook, stirring occasionally, until the liquid starts to thicken, about 10 minutes. Stir in the apple cider, broth, vinegar, and thyme and season with salt and pepper. Bring to a boil.

SLOW COOK Transfer the insert to the slow cooker and add the pork. Cover and cook on the low-heat setting for 8 hours. The pork should be tender.

Uncover and cook on the high-heat setting, basting frequently with the cooking liquid, for 1 hour longer.

ASSEMBLE Transfer the pork to a cutting board and tent with aluminum foil to keep warm. Remove and discard the thyme from the cooking liquid. Using a large spoon, skim off and discard as much fat as possible from the surface of the liquid. Using a large, sharp knife, cut the pork across the grain into thin slices.

SERVE Arrange the slices on a platter, spoon the braising liquid over the top, and serve right away.

Italian-Style Braised Pork

In this traditional recipe from northern Italy, the natural sugars in the milk complement the sweetness of the pork, and the liquid cooks down to form a thick sauce. Serve with mashed potatoes and sautéed greens, such as kale or chard.

ingredients

1 boneless pork loin roast,
2–2½ lb (1–1.25 kg)

Kosher salt and freshly ground pepper

2 tablespoons olive oil

3 slices thick-cut bacon, about 3 oz (90 g) total weight, coarsely chopped

3–4 cups (24–32 fl oz/750 ml–1 l) whole milk

6 sage leaves

4 cloves garlic

2 wide strips lemon peel

makes 6–8 servings

step by step

PREP Season the pork generously with salt and pepper.

BUILD FLAVOR Put the slow-cooker insert on the stove top over medium heat, then add the oil and warm until hot. Add the bacon and fry, stirring often, until browned, 2–3 minutes. Using a slotted spoon, transfer to paper towels to drain. Raise the heat to medium-high. Add the pork to the fat remaining in the insert and cook, turning as needed, until browned on all sides, about 10 minutes. Transfer to a plate and set aside. Pour off the fat from the insert and return the insert to medium-high heat. Pour in 3 cups (24 fl oz/750 ml) of the milk and deglaze the insert, stirring and scraping up the browned bits on the insert bottom with a wooden spoon. Bring to a boil.

SLOW COOK Transfer the insert to the slow cooker and add the pork, bacon, sage, garlic, and lemon peel. Cover and cook on the low-heat setting for 6 hours. The pork should be tender. During the last 1–2 hours of cooking, check the milk level; if it seems like it has evaporated too much, warm remaining 1 cup (8 fl oz/250 ml) milk in a saucepan until steaming, add it to the slow cooker, and continue to cook.

ASSEMBLE Transfer the pork to a cutting board and tent with aluminum foil to keep warm. Remove and discard the sage, garlic cloves, and lemon peel from the cooking liquid. Leave the liquid in the slow cooker and turn the heat to high, or pour it into a saucepan and place over high heat. Cook the liquid, whisking constantly, until a thick sauce forms, about 5 minutes on the stove top or 10 minutes in the slow cooker.

Cut the pork across the grain into slices about ½ inch (12 mm) thick.

SERVE Arrange the pork slices on a platter, top with the sauce, and serve right away.

Japanese Pork Curry

Japanese-style curries have a milder flavor than traditional Indian-style curries and there are as many recipes as there are grandmothers. I'm particularly partial to this version, with lots of tender pork, buttery potatoes, and earthy carrots in a tangy, slightly sweet sauce. Serve this over steamed rice, as is traditional, or just on its own.

ingredients

3 lb (1.5 kg) pork shoulder, cut into 3 pieces

Kosher salt

2 tablespoons canola oil

1 yellow onion, halved lengthwise and thinly sliced

3 cloves garlic, minced

1 tablespoon grated fresh ginger

¼ cup (1 oz/30 g) all-purposed flour

2 tablespoons mild yellow curry powder

2 tablespoons tomato paste or ketchup

2 tablespoons Worcestershire sauce

1 tablespoon honey

3 cups (24 fl oz/750 ml) low-sodium chicken or vegetable broth

1 lb (500 g) Yukon Gold potatoes, cut into 1-inch (2.5-cm) pieces

2 carrots, peeled, halved lengthwise, and sliced on the diagonal

1 large apple, such as Pink Lady, peeled, cored, and grated

1 can (13½ oz/425 g) coconut milk, shaken well before opening

makes 8 servings

step by step

PREP Season the pork all over with salt.

BUILD FLAVOR (OPTIONAL) Put the slow-cooker insert on the stove top over medium-high heat, then add the oil and warm until hot. Working in batches if necessary to avoid crowding, add the pork pieces and sear them on the first side without moving them until well browned, 3–4 minutes. Turn the pieces and sear on the second side until well browned, 3–4 minutes longer. Transfer the pork pieces to a plate.

QUICK COOK If you have included the browning step, pour off all but 1 tablespoon of the fat from the insert. If you are starting here, put the slow-cooker insert on the stove top over medium-high heat, then add the oil and warm until hot. Add the onion, garlic, and ginger, sprinkle with a pinch or salt, and cook, stirring, for 3 minutes. Sprinkle in the flour and cook, stirring, for 2 minutes. Stir in the curry powder, tomato paste, Worcestershire sauce, honey, and 1 teaspoon salt. Slowly pour in 1 cup (8 fl oz/250 ml) of the chicken broth, and deglaze the insert, stirring and scraping up the browned bits on the insert bottom with a wooden spoon until the mixture is smooth. Stir in the remaining 2 cups (16 fl oz/500 ml) broth until mixed. Bring to a boil.

SLOW COOK Transfer the insert to the slow cooker and add the pork. Cover and cook on the low-heat setting for 4 hours.

Add the potatoes, carrots, and apple, then cover and cook on the low-heat setting for 4 hours. The pork and vegetables will be tender.

ASSEMBLE Using a large spoon, skim off any fat from the top of the cooking liquid. Transfer the pork to a cutting board. Using 2 forks, break the pork into large chunks, discarding any large pieces of fat. Return the meat to the slow cooker along with the coconut milk and stir gently to combine. Cover and cook on the low-heat setting for 30 minutes to warm through. Taste and season with salt.

SERVE Divide the curry among individual bowls and serve right away.

Sweet-n-Tangy Pork Ribs

Here, a quick, made-from-scratch simmering sauce imparts complex flavors to meaty country-style pork ribs. The sauce is also good paired with other meats, such as beef brisket or bone-in chicken thighs. The latter will cook in just 4–6 hours. Round out the menu with cole slaw and buttery corn on the cob.

ingredients

1 yellow onion, finely chopped

½ cup (4 fl oz/125 ml) low-sodium beef or chicken broth

½ cup (4 oz/125 g) tomato ketchup

¼ cup (2 oz/60 g) Dijon mustard

¼ cup (2 fl oz/60 ml) Worcestershire sauce

3 tablespoons rice or cider vinegar

2 tablespoons low-sodium soy sauce

3 tablespoons firmly packed dark brown sugar

1 teaspoon dry mustard

1 teaspoon ground cumin

1 teaspoon ground coriander

Hot-pepper sauce for seasoning

3½ lb (1.75 kg) country-style pork ribs

Kosher salt and freshly ground pepper

makes 6 servings

step by step

PREP To make a sauce, in a bowl, combine the onion, broth, ketchup, Dijon mustard, Worcestershire sauce, vinegar, soy sauce, sugar, dry mustard, cumin, and coriander and stir to mix well. Season with the hot-pepper sauce. The sauce can be covered and refrigerated for up to 2 days before using.

Season the pork ribs generously with salt and pepper.

BUILD FLAVOR (OPTIONAL) Preheat the broiler. Arrange the ribs in a single layer of a rimmed baking sheet. Broil, turning the ribs at the midpoint, until well browned on both sides, 10–15 minutes.

SLOW COOK Transfer the ribs to the slow cooker and pour the sauce over them. Turn the ribs to coat them evenly with the sauce. Cover and cook on the low-heat setting for 8 hours. The ribs should be very tender.

ASSEMBLE Transfer the ribs to a platter and cover to keep warm. Using a large spoon, skim off and discard any fat from the surface of the sauce. Then, if desired, strain the sauce through a fine-mesh sieve into a small saucepan, put the pan over medium-high heat, and boil until syrupy, about 5 minutes.

SERVE Pour the sauce over the ribs and serve right away.

Five-Spice Spareribs

Fall-apart tender, these pork ribs are braised in a sweet-salty hoisin-based sauce.
For a spicier result, add 2—3 tablespoons Sriracha to the hoisin mixture. It will take
a few minutes to reduce the sauce before serving, but the extra time adds a
welcome flavor intensity to the dish. Serve the ribs with plenty of steamed rice.

ingredients

4—4½ lb (2—2.25 kg) pork spareribs
(1½—2 racks), back membrane
removed and racks cut in half
crosswise by the butcher

Kosher salt and freshly ground pepper

1 cup (8 fl oz/250 ml) fresh orange juice

½ cup (4 fl oz/125 ml) hoisin sauce

¼ cup (2 fl oz/60 ml) low-sodium soy sauce

3 cloves garlic, minced

1 tablespoon peeled and grated
fresh ginger

1 teaspoon five-spice powder

makes 6 servings

step by step

PREP Season the ribs with salt and a generous amount of pepper.

BUILD FLAVOR (OPTIONAL) Preheat the broiler. Arrange the rib racks, bone side down, on a rimmed baking sheet. Broil until nicely browned on one side, 10—15 minutes. Remove the racks from the broiler, let them cool until they can be handled, and then cut the racks into individual ribs.

SLOW COOK In the slow cooker, combine the orange juice, hoisin sauce, soy sauce, garlic, ginger, and five-spice powder and stir to mix well. If you have skipped the broiling step, cut the racks into individual ribs. Add the ribs and toss to coat with the sauce. Cover and cook on the low-heat setting for 8 hours. Turn the ribs in the sauce once or twice as they cook. They should be very tender when they are done.

ASSEMBLE Transfer the ribs to a platter and cover to keep warm. Using a large spoon, skim off and discard any fat from the surface of the sauce. Then, if desired, strain the sauce through a fine-mesh sieve into a small saucepan, put the pan over medium-high heat, and boil until syrupy, about 5 minutes.

SERVE Pour the sauce over the ribs and serve right away.

Barbecue-Style Baby Back Ribs

Craving the flavors of a backyard barbecue but the weather is not cooperating?
This is the recipe for you. The sauce is made the night before from a handful of pantry
staples. You can prep the ribs at the same time. Then, when it's time to cook, a quick
stint under the broiler preps the ribs for a long, slow braise in the barbecue sauce.
Serve these with creamy potato salad and baked beans to complete the barbecue theme.

ingredients

1 tablespoon canola oil

½ yellow onion, finely chopped

3 cloves garlic, minced

1 cup (8 oz/250 g) tomato ketchup

3 tablespoons Worcestershire sauce

3 tablespoons dry white wine

½ teaspoon grated lemon zest

1½ tablespoons fresh lemon juice

1½ tablespoons firmly packed dark brown sugar

1½ teaspoons dry mustard

1½ teaspoons chipotle chile powder

1 teaspoon ground cumin

¼ teaspoon celery salt

Kosher salt

1 teaspoon hot-pepper sauce

5 lb (2.5 kg) baby back ribs

makes 6 servings

step by step

PREP Up to 24 hours before you plan to start cooking, in a saucepan over medium heat, warm the oil. Add the onion and garlic and cook, stirring, until softened, about 5 minutes. Add the ketchup, Worcestershire sauce, wine, lemon zest and juice, brown sugar, mustard, chile powder, cumin, celery salt, and ½ teaspoon salt and stir to mix well. Bring to a simmer, then reduce the heat to low and cook very gently, stirring occasionally to prevent scorching, until slightly thickened, 12—15 minutes. Stir in the hot-pepper sauce and taste and adjust the seasoning with more salt and pepper sauce if needed. Transfer the sauce to a bowl, let cool, cover, and refrigerate until ready to use.

Trim the membrane from the back of each rib rack, then cut the racks into individual ribs. Store in a zippered plastic bag or airtight container for up to 24 hours.

BUILD FLAVOR Preheat the broiler. Put a wire rack in a rimmed baking sheet and arrange the ribs on the rack. Broil, turning once, until browned on both sides, 10—12 minutes total.

SLOW COOK Transfer the ribs to the slow cooker, add the barbecue sauce, and turn the ribs to coat evenly. Cover and cook on the low-heat setting for 5—6 hours. The ribs should be very tender.

ASSEMBLE Using a slotted spatula, transfer the ribs to a large platter and cover to keep warm. Pour the sauce remaining in the insert into a small saucepan, let stand for few minutes, and then, using a large spoon, skim off and discard the fat from the surface. Place over high heat, bring to a boil, and boil rapidly to reduce and thicken slightly, 3—4 minutes.

SERVE Arrange the ribs on individual plates and drizzle with reduced sauce. Serve right away.

Maple-Braised Pork Chops

Pork chops take well to sweet flavors, and this dish, an ode to New England, balances the dark sweetness of maple syrup with a little punch of chile powder and cider vinegar. Serve these tender chops with sautéed hearty greens and roasted sweet potatoes or regular potatoes.

ingredients

3 tablespoons all-purpose flour

Kosher salt and freshly ground pepper

6 bone-in pork loin chops, each about 12 oz (375 g) and 1½ inches (4 cm) thick

2 tablespoons canola oil

1 small yellow onion, finely chopped

1 clove garlic, minced

2 teaspoons chile powder

¾ cup (6 fl oz/180 ml) low-sodium chicken broth

¾ cup (8 oz/250 g) maple syrup

3 tablespoons cider vinegar

2 tablespoons Worcestershire sauce

2 tablespoons finely chopped fresh chives

makes 6 servings

step by step

PREP On a plate, stir together the flour, ¾ teaspoon salt, and ½ teaspoon pepper. Turn the pork chops in the seasoned flour, coating evenly and shaking off any excess.

BUILD FLAVOR (OPTIONAL) Put the slow-cooker insert on the stove top over medium-high heat, then add the oil and warm until hot. Working in batches if necessary to avoid crowding, add the pork chops and cook, turning once, until golden brown on both sides, about 4 minutes on each side. Transfer to a plate and set aside.

QUICK COOK If you have included the browning step, pour off all but 2 tablespoons of the fat from the insert and return the insert to medium-high heat. If you are starting here, put the slow-cooker insert on the stove top over medium-high heat, then add the oil and warm until hot. Add the onion, garlic, and chile powder and cook, stirring, until fragrant, 30–60 seconds. Pour in the broth and deglaze the insert, stirring and scraping up the browned bits on the insert bottom with a wooden spoon. Stir in the maple syrup, vinegar, and Worcestershire sauce and bring to a boil.

SLOW COOK Transfer the insert to the slow cooker, add the pork chops, and turn the chops to coat evenly. Cover and cook on the low-heat setting for 8 hours. The chops should be tender.

SERVE Transfer the chops to individual plates and spoon the cooking liquid over the top. Garnish with the chives and serve right away.

Orange-Glazed Ham

This beautifully glazed ham is deceptively dramatic, especially considering how simple it is to make. Cutting a diamond pattern over the top and sides takes just minutes and cooks into an elegant finish. Serve this holiday-appropriate main dish with roasted asparagus and scalloped potatoes.

ingredients

1 cured ham from the shank end,
7–8 lb (3.5–4 kg)

2 cups (16 fl oz/500 ml) fresh orange juice

1 tablespoon grated orange zest

1 cup (7 oz/220 g) firmly packed golden brown sugar

1 cinnamon stick, broken in half

6 whole cloves

6 peppercorns

makes 8–10 servings

step by step

PREP Using a large, sharp knife, remove the skin from the ham if necessary and trim the fat, leaving a layer ½ inch (12 mm) thick. Score the top and sides of the ham at 1-inch (2.5-cm) intervals to form a diamond pattern.

QUICK COOK Put the slow-cooker insert on the stove top over medium heat, add the orange juice and zest, sugar, cinnamon, cloves, and peppercorns. Cook, stirring frequently, until the mixture is thick and syrupy, about 15 minutes. Transfer the glaze to a small bowl and set aside.

SLOW COOK Transfer the insert to the slow cooker. Place the ham, fat side up, in the slow cooker. Cover and cook on the low-heat setting for 6 hours.

Uncover and use a spoon to remove most of the fat from the bottom of the insert. Pour the glaze over the ham, re-cover, and continue to cook on the low-heat setting until the juices around the ham are bubbling and the top of the ham is glistening, about 2 hours longer.

ASSEMBLE Transfer the ham to a cutting board, tent with aluminum foil, and let rest for 15 minutes. Using a large, sharp knife, cut the ham across the grain into thin slices.

SERVE Arrange the slices on a platter and serve right away.

Easy Cassoulet
with
Sausage, Bacon, and Riesling

This quick-to-assemble version of a traditional French cassoulet features smoked sausage, thick-cut bacon, and creamy white beans. Pour the remainder of the wine with the meal, and accompany with a salad with a mustard vinaigrette.

ingredients

1 lb (500 g) thick-cut bacon slices, finely chopped

1 lb (500 g) fully cooked smoked pork sausages such as kielbasa

1 carrot, peeled and finely chopped

1 yellow onion, finely chopped

1 teaspoon minced garlic

¼ cup (1½ oz/45 g) all-purpose flour

2 tablespoons Dijon mustard

1 cup (8 fl oz/250 ml) Riesling or other fruity white wine

1 cup (8 fl oz/250 ml) low-sodium chicken broth

2 tablespoons firmly packed dark brown sugar

½ teaspoon ground coriander

¼ teaspoon ground cloves

Freshly ground pepper

2 cans (15 oz/470 g each) white beans, drained and rinsed

makes 4–6 servings

step by step

QUICK COOK Put the slow-cooker insert on the stove top over medium heat, then add the bacon and fry, stirring occasionally, until the fat is rendered, about 10 minutes. With a slotted spoon, transfer the bacon to a plate. Raise the heat to medium-high, and add the sausages. Cook the sausages, turning them as needed, until evenly browned, about 4 minutes total. Transfer the sausages to a plate with the bacon.

Carefully pour off all but 2 tablespoons of the fat from the insert and return the insert to medium-high heat. Add the carrot, onion, and garlic and sauté until softened, 3–5 minutes. Whisk in the flour and mustard and cook, stirring, until the flour is fully incorporated, 30–60 seconds. Pour in the wine and simmer until it evaporates, about 2 minutes. Whisk in the broth, sugar, coriander, cloves, and a few grinds of pepper and bring to a boil.

SLOW COOK Transfer the insert to the slow cooker, add the beans, sausages, and bacon and stir to mix. Cover and cook on the low-heat setting for 3 hours. The sausages should be heated through and tender.

SERVE Spoon the cassoulet onto a serving platter and serve right away.

Chicken

Thai Coconut Chicken Soup

One of my favorite Thai take-out dishes is the chicken-coconut soup known as tom kha gai. But you can put together a great version at home in no more time than it takes you to pick up an order at a restaurant. This recipe is packed with flavor: tender chicken breast, braised mushrooms, earthy spinach, and a lime-spiked creamy coconut broth.

ingredients

4 lb (2 kg) bone-in chicken breast halves, skinned (4–5 breast halves)

Kosher salt

2 cups (16 fl oz/500 ml) low-sodium chicken broth

Grated zest and juice of 1 lime, plus more lime juice, if needed

3 tablespoons Asian fish sauce

2 tablespoons firmly packed golden brown sugar

1 jalapeño chile, thinly sliced (optional)

¾ lb (375 g) button or small cremini mushrooms, brushed clean and halved or quartered

2 cans (13½ fl oz/420 ml each) coconut milk, shaken well before opening

1 can (8 oz/250 g) sliced bamboo shoots, drained and rinsed (optional)

⅓ lb (5 oz/155 g) baby spinach (optional)

⅓ cup (⅓ oz/10 g) fresh cilantro leaves, chopped, plus more for garnish

Chopped green onions, white and pale green parts, for garnish

makes 6–8 servings

step by step

PREP Season the chicken with salt.

SLOW COOK In a slow cooker, combine the broth, the zest and juice of 1 lime, the fish sauce, and the sugar and stir to dissolve the sugar. Add the chicken, bone side up, in a single layer, if possible. Scatter the jalapeño, if using, and then the mushrooms evenly over the chicken. Cover and cook on the low-heat setting for 4 hours. The chicken should be tender and opaque throughout.

Uncover and transfer the chicken to a cutting board. When just cool enough to handle, bone the chicken and discard the bones and any errant fat or gristle. Shred the meat with your fingers or 2 forks and return it to the slow cooker. Add the coconut milk, the bamboo shoots and spinach (if using), and the cilantro and stir well. Re-cover and continue to cook on the low-heat setting, stirring occasionally, until the chicken is heated through, the spinach is cooked, and the flavors have blended, 30–60 minutes.

SERVE Taste and adjust the seasoning with lime juice and salt if needed. Ladle the soup into individual bowls and garnish with cilantro and green onions. Serve right away.

Lemon Chicken
and
Rice Soup

This is my go-to recipe when I feel a cold coming on. I like to steam the rice separately to keep it from getting mushy. Also, if you cook the rice separately, you can easily freeze the soup and then cook the rice when you are ready to serve the soup. For chicken-noodle soup, omit the rice and lemon and add cooked egg noodles to the finished soup.

ingredients

2½ lb (1.25 kg) bone-in chicken thighs, skinned (about 6 large thighs)

2 carrots, peeled and finely diced

2 ribs celery, finely diced

2 leeks, white and pale green part, trimmed, quartered lengthwise, and thinly sliced (about 2½ cups/7½ oz/235 g)

2 sprigs fresh thyme

7–8 cups (56–64 fl oz/1.75–2 l) low-sodium chicken broth

Kosher salt

Juice of 1 large lemon

1 cup (7 oz/220 g) long-grain white rice

makes 6–8 servings

step by step

SLOW COOK In the slow cooker, combine the chicken, carrots, celery, leeks, thyme, 7 cups (56 fl oz/1.75 l) of the broth, and 2 teaspoons salt and stir to mix well. Cover and cook on the low-heat setting for 4 hours. The chicken should be very tender and opaque throughout.

ASSEMBLE Transfer the chicken to a cutting board. When just cool enough to handle, bone the chicken and discard the bones and any errant fat or gristle. Shred the meat into bite-size chunks with your fingers or 2 forks. Return the chicken to the slow cooker, add the lemon juice, and stir well. If you like a brothier soup, stir in the remaining 1 cup (8 fl oz/250 ml) broth. Re-cover and cook on the low-heat setting for about 20 minutes to warm the chicken through.

While the chicken is reheating, steam the rice in a rice cooker or according to your favorite stove-top method. Stir the cooked rice into the soup.

SERVE Ladle the soup into individual bowls and serve right away.

Five-Spice Chicken Pho

This Vietnamese-style chicken soup is bursting with layers of flavor. The broth—infused with star anise, cinnamon, and five-spice powder—is a snap to throw together, and the chicken picks up all of the flavors of the spices as it slowly simmers. Here, the soup is ladled over rice noodles, but it can also be served without the noodles.

ingredients

8 cups (64 fl oz/2 l) low-sodium chicken broth

1 yellow onion, halved and sliced

3 tablespoons Asian fish sauce

2 cinnamon sticks

4 star anise pods

2-inch (5-cm) piece fresh ginger, peeled and thinly sliced

1 teaspoon five-spice powder

½ teaspoon ground coriander

2 teaspoons sugar

Kosher salt

2½ lb (1.25 kg) bone-in chicken thighs, skinned (about 6 large thighs)

¾ lb (375 g) dried rice noodles, about ⅛ inch (3 mm) wide

Bean sprouts, thinly sliced jalapeño chiles, lime wedges, fresh Thai or sweet basil, cilantro, and/or mint leaves Sriracha sauce, and hoisin sauce for serving

makes 6 servings

step by step

SLOW COOK In a slow cooker, stir together the broth, onion, fish sauce, cinnamon, star anise, ginger, five-spice powder, coriander, sugar, and 1 teaspoon salt. Add the chicken, cover, and cook on the low-heat setting for 6 hours. The chicken should be very tender and opaque throughout.

ASSEMBLE Transfer the chicken to a cutting board. When just cool enough to handle, bone the chicken and discard the bones and any fat or gristle. Shred the meat into bite-size chunks with your fingers or 2 forks. Line a fine-mesh sieve with cheesecloth and strain the broth through the sieve into a bowl; discard the solids. Return the broth and the shredded chicken to the slow cooker, cover, and cook on the low-heat setting for 30 minutes to warm through.

While the broth and meat are reheating, prepare the rice noodles according to package directions. Arrange the bean sprouts, chiles, lime wedges, and herb leaves on a platter and set on the table along with the Sriracha and hoisin sauces.

SERVE Divide the rice noodles evenly among individual bowls and ladle the hot broth and chicken over the noodles. Invite diners to top their soup with the herbs, sprouts, chiles, lime juice, and sauces as desired.

Spanish-Style Chicken Stew

Olives and almonds are staples of Spanish cuisine. In this versatile, boldly flavored dish, I've combined them with a whole, cut-up chicken, sweet peppers, tomatoes, and garlic. To save time, toast the almonds the night before and store them in an airtight container at room temperature. Serve the stew with roasted potatoes.

ingredients

1 chicken, 4–5 lb (2–2.5 kg), cut into 8 serving pieces, trimmed of excess skin and fat

Kosher salt and freshly ground pepper

2 tablespoons unsalted butter, if including the optional browning step

2 tablespoons canola oil

2 red or yellow bell peppers, seeded and finely chopped

1 yellow onion, thinly sliced

1 clove garlic, minced

2 tomatoes, seeded and chopped

2 teaspoons hot smoked paprika

1 can (15 oz/470 g) chickpeas, drained and rinsed

¾ cup (4 oz/125 g) pitted green olives

½ cup (2 oz/60 g) sliced almonds, toasted, plus more for garnish

makes 4–6 servings

step by step

PREP Season the chicken with salt and pepper.

BUILD FLAVOR (OPTIONAL) Put the slow-cooker insert on the stove top over medium-high heat, then add the butter and oil and warm until hot. Working in batches to avoid crowding, add the chicken pieces and cook, turning as needed, until browned, 7–10 minutes. Transfer to a plate and set aside.

QUICK COOK If you have included the browning step, pour off all but 2 tablespoons of the fat from the insert and return the insert to medium-high heat. If you are starting here, put the slow-cooker insert on the stove top over medium-high heat, then add the oil and warm until hot. Add the bell peppers and onion and sauté until softened, about 5 minutes. Add the garlic and cook, stirring, for 1 minute. Stir in the tomatoes and paprika.

SLOW COOK Transfer the insert to the slow cooker, add the chicken and chickpeas, and stir and turn the chicken to coat evenly with the bell pepper mixture. Cover and cook on the low-heat setting for 5½ hours. The chicken should be tender and opaque throughout.

Uncover and add the olives and almonds, distributing them evenly. Re-cover and cook on the low-heat setting for about 30 minutes longer, until the stew is fragrant.

SERVE Transfer the stew to a wide, shallow serving bowl. Garnish with almonds and serve right away.

Chicken Enchilada Stew

Start this dish in the late morning, and by dinnertime you'll have a hearty, comforting Mexican-style stew. Serve this with a green salad with avocado and a citrus vinaigrette. Don't skip the garnishes for the stew—the contrast of melting cheese and crunchy chips adds flavor and texture to the dish.

ingredients

2 cans (15 oz/470 g each) diced fire-roasted tomatoes with juice

1 can (15 oz/470 g) black beans, drained and rinsed

2 cans (4 oz/125 g each) diced mild green chiles, drained

1 yellow onion, finely chopped

2½ cups (20 fl oz/625 ml) low-sodium chicken broth

2 tablespoons chili powder

2 teaspoons ground cumin

Grated zest and juice of 1 lime, plus more juice to taste if needed and lime wedges for serving

Kosher salt

2½ lb (1.25 kg) bone-in chicken thighs, skinned (about 6 large thighs)

¼ cup (⅓ oz/10 g) finely chopped fresh cilantro

Shredded Monterey jack or Cheddar cheese for garnish

Tortilla chips for garnish

makes 6–8 servings

step by step

SLOW COOK In the slow cooker, combine the tomatoes, beans, chiles, onion, broth, chili powder, cumin, zest and juice of 1 lime, and 2 teaspoons salt and stir to mix well. Nestle the chicken thighs in the tomato mixture. Cover and cook on the low-heat setting for 6 hours. The chicken should be very tender and opaque throughout.

ASSEMBLE Transfer the chicken to a cutting board. When just cool enough to handle, bone the chicken and discard the bones and any fat or gristle. Using your fingers or 2 forks, shred the meat into large bite-size pieces. Return the meat to the slow cooker, add the cilantro, and stir to mix well. Taste and adjust the seasoning with more salt or lime juice if needed. Cover and continue to cook on the low-heat setting for 30 minutes to warm the chicken through.

SERVE Divide the stew among individual bowls, top each serving with some cheese and a few chips, and serve right away. Pass the lime wedges at the table.

Chicken Korma

Rich and mild, this slow-simmered northern Indian curry has complex flavors that belie the amount of effort it takes to make it. The sauce is thickened by puréeing cashews with buttermilk and then stirring the mixture into the braising liquid, yielding an ultracreamy texture. Serve with steamed basmati rice to soak up the sauce.

ingredients

¼ cup (2 fl oz/60 ml) canola oil

1 yellow onion, finely chopped

2 cloves garlic, minced

2-inch (5-cm) piece fresh ginger, peeled and grated

2-inch (5-cm) piece cinnamon stick

2 bay leaves

1 tablespoon ground coriander

1 teaspoon ground turmeric

½ teaspoon cayenne pepper

½ teaspoon ground cumin

1½ cups (12 fl oz/375 ml) low-sodium chicken broth

1 cup (8 fl oz/250 ml) tomato sauce

1 tablespoon sugar

Kosher salt

3 lb (1.5 kg) bone-in chicken breast halves (3–4 breast halves)

½ cup (4 fl oz/125 ml) buttermilk

½ cup (3 oz/90 g) toasted cashew nuts

3 tablespoons chopped fresh cilantro

makes 6–8 servings

step by step

QUICK COOK Put the slow-cooker insert on the stove top over medium-high heat, then add the oil and warm until hot. Add the onion and cook, stirring, until it begins to soften, about 3 minutes. Add the garlic, ginger, cinnamon, bay leaves, coriander, turmeric, cayenne, and cumin and cook, stirring, until the spices are fragrant and evenly coat the onion, about 1 minute. Stir in the broth, tomato sauce, sugar, and 1 teaspoon salt and deglaze the insert, stirring and scraping up the browned bits on the insert bottom with a wooden spoon. Bring to a boil.

SLOW COOK Transfer the insert to the slow cooker. Add the chicken and turn to coat with the broth mixture. Cover and cook on the low-heat setting for 4 hours. The chicken should be very tender and opaque throughout.

Uncover and transfer the chicken to a cutting board. When just cool enough to handle, bone the chicken and discard the bones and any fat or gristle. Shred the meat with your fingers or 2 forks and return it to the slow cooker. Re-cover and continue to cook on the low-heat setting, stirring occasionally, until the chicken is heated through.

ASSEMBLE About 15 minutes before the chicken is ready, combine the buttermilk and cashews in a blender or food processor and process until the nuts are finely puréed and thoroughly mixed with the buttermilk. Add to the chicken and stir to mix well. Re-cover and continue to cook on the low-heat setting until the sauce is heated through and thick, about 5 minutes. Remove and discard the cinnamon stick and bay leaves.

SERVE Divide the chicken and sauce evenly among individual bowls, garnish with the cilantro, and serve right away.

Vietnamese Yellow Chicken Curry

In this recipe, as with many curries in Southeast Asia, coconut milk is used
as the primary cooking liquid, lending a rich flavor and creamy texture.
Chunks of tender sweet potato and carrots lend a slight sweetness to
the dish, and all you need to round out the menu is steamed jasmine rice.

ingredients

2 tablespoons canola oil

3 lb (1.5 kg) bone-in chicken thighs, skinned

3 cloves garlic, minced

2 shallots, minced

3 tablespoons Madras-style curry powder

1 tablespoon firmly packed dark brown sugar

1 teaspoon red pepper flakes

Freshly ground black pepper

2 stalks lemongrass, tender bulb part only, trimmed, tough outer layers discarded, and cut into 1-inch (2.5-cm) pieces

1-inch (2.5-cm) piece fresh ginger, peeled and cut into 4 equal slices

1 cup (8 fl oz/250 ml) low-sodium chicken broth

1 can (13½ fl oz/420 ml) coconut milk, shaken well before opening

2 tablespoons Asian fish sauce

3 carrots, peeled and cut into 1-inch (2.5-cm) chunks

1 sweet potato, about ¾ lb (375 g), peeled and cut into 1-inch (2.5-cm) chunks

3 tablespoons finely shredded fresh Thai or sweet basil

makes 6–8 servings

step by step

BUILD FLAVOR (OPTIONAL) Put the slow-cooker insert on the stove top over medium-high heat, then add the oil and warm until hot. Working in batches if necessary to avoid crowding, add the chicken thighs and cook, turning once, until nicely browned on both sides, about 4 minutes on each side. Transfer to a plate and set aside.

QUICK COOK If you have included the browning step, pour off all but 2 tablespoons of the fat and return the insert to medium-high heat. If you are starting here, put the slow-cooker insert on the stove top over medium-high heat, then add the oil and warm until hot. Add the garlic and shallots and cook, stirring, just until fragrant, about 30 seconds. Add the curry powder, sugar, pepper flakes, 1 teaspoon black pepper, the lemongrass, and the ginger and cook, stirring, until the spices are fragrant and evenly coat the garlic and shallots, about 30 seconds. Pour in the broth and deglaze the insert, stirring and scraping up the browned bits on the insert bottom with a wooden spoon. Stir in the coconut milk and fish sauce and bring to a boil.

SLOW COOK Transfer the insert to the slow cooker. Add the chicken, carrots, and sweet potato, pushing them into the liquid. Cover and cook on the low-heat setting for 6 hours. The chicken should be tender and opaque throughout.

SERVE Transfer the curry to a shallow serving bowl. Garnish with the basil and serve right away.

Thai Green Curry Chicken

Curry pastes can range in spiciness, so choose one with a heat level that suits your tastes. The one I use in this recipe is mild to medium. If yours is quite spicy, use only 1 tablespoon. When the dish is ready, the sauce may look as if it has separated. Just give it a quick stir and it will come together. Serve this full-flavored curry with plenty of rice.

ingredients

2½ lb (1.25 kg) bone-in chicken thighs, skinned (about 6 large thighs)

Kosher salt

Grated zest and juice of 2 limes

3 tablespoons Asian fish sauce

2 tablespoons firmly packed golden brown sugar

1-2 tablespoons green curry paste

4 cloves garlic, chopped

½ yellow onion, coarsely chopped

½ cup (½ oz/15 g) fresh cilantro leaves, chopped, plus more for garnish

1 can (13½ fl oz/420 ml) coconut milk, shaken well before opening

1 cup (8 fl oz/250 ml) low-sodium chicken broth

½ lb (250 g) green beans, trimmed and cut into 1-inch (2.5-cm) pieces

1 red bell pepper, seeded and cut into thin slices about 1 inch (2.5 cm) long (about 1 cup/5 oz/155 g)

4 green onions, white and pale green parts, sliced

makes 6—8 servings

step by step

PREP Put the chicken on a plate and sprinkle evenly on both sides with about 1½ teaspoons salt and the zest of 1 lime. Cover and set aside at room temperature for at least 30 minutes or up to overnight in the refrigerator.

In a blender, combine the fish sauce, sugar, curry paste to taste, garlic, yellow onion, the remaining zest of 1 lime and the juice of 2 limes, and half of the cilantro and process until a smooth purée forms.

SLOW COOK Pour the puréed onion mixture into the slow cooker, add the coconut milk and broth, and whisk to combine. Add the chicken thighs, submerging them in the liquid. Cover and cook on the low-heat setting for 4 hours. The chicken should be very tender and opaque throughout.

Uncover and transfer the chicken to a cutting board. Meanwhile, add the green beans, bell pepper, and green onions to the slow cooker and stir to coat with the sauce. Re-cover and continue to cook on the low-heat setting for 45 minutes. The vegetables should be tender.

ASSEMBLE While the vegetables are cooking, bone the chicken and discard the bones and any fat or gristle. Using your fingers, break up the meat into large pieces. When the vegetables are ready, return the chicken to the slow cooker, add the remaining cilantro, and stir well. Re-cover and continue to cook on the low-heat setting for about 15 minutes to warm the chicken through.

SERVE Transfer the curry to a serving bowl and serve right away.

Easy Chicken Mole

You can use this same sauce with bone-in turkey breast, which is traditional, or pork shoulder or beef chuck. You can also de-bone the cooked thighs, shred the meat, stir it into the sauce, and use it as a taco, enchilada, or burrito filling. Offer a salad of sliced oranges, red onions, and avocado alongside.

ingredients

1½ cups (9 oz/280 g) crushed fire-roasted tomatoes with juice

1 yellow onion, finely chopped

¼ cup (1½ oz/45 g) chipotle chiles in adobo sauce

¼ cup (1 oz/30 g) almonds or walnuts

¼ cup (1½ oz/45 g) raisins

1 oz (30 g) bittersweet chocolate, finely chopped

3 tablespoons canola oil

1 tablespoon fresh orange juice

1 clove garlic, coarsely chopped

½ teaspoon ground cumin

½ teaspoon dried oregano

½ teaspoon ground cinnamon

Kosher salt and freshly ground pepper

6 large bone-in chicken thighs, about 2½ lb (1.25 kg) total weight, skinned

makes 6 servings

step by step

PREP In a food processor, combine the tomatoes, onion, chipotle chiles and sauce, nuts, raisins, chocolate, oil, orange juice, garlic, cumin, oregano, cinnamon, ½ teaspoon salt, and a few grinds of pepper and process until smooth, about 1 minute.

SLOW COOK Put the chicken in the slow cooker and sprinkle evenly with ¼ teaspoon salt. Pour the tomato mixture evenly over the top. Cover and cook on the low-heat setting for 6 hours. The chicken should be tender and opaque throughout.

SERVE Divide the chicken among individual plates. Stir the sauce until smooth, spoon over the chicken, and serve right away.

Chicken Adobo

Like the Beef Adobo on page 32, this quick and easy recipe celebrates the classic adobo of the Philippines. The dark, rich meat of chicken thighs works especially well with the robust flavors—vinegar, soy sauce, garlic—of the cooking liquid. Serve with steamed rice and a salad of tomatoes and cucumbers.

ingredients

2 yellow onions, halved and thinly sliced

1-inch (2.5-cm) piece fresh ginger, peeled and cut into 4 equal slices

6 cloves garlic, crushed

3–3½ lb (1.5–1.75 kg) bone-in chicken thighs, skinned (about 8 thighs)

Kosher salt and freshly ground pepper

¾ cup (6 fl oz/180 ml) white wine vinegar

½ cup (4 fl oz/125 ml) low-sodium soy sauce

1 tablespoon sugar

2 limes, cut into wedges

makes 6–8 servings

step by step

PREP Spread half of the onion slices evenly in the bottom of the slow cooker. Top with the ginger and garlic, distributing them evenly. Arrange the chicken pieces in a single layer over the onions. Sprinkle with ¼ teaspoon salt and 1 teaspoon pepper and cover the chicken evenly with the remaining onion slices. Drizzle evenly with the vinegar and soy sauce and sprinkle with the sugar.

SLOW COOK Cover and cook on the low-heat setting for 6 hours. The chicken should be tender and opaque throughout.

ASSEMBLE Remove and discard the ginger slices and garlic cloves. Using a large spoon, skim and discard any fat from the surface of the cooking liquid.

SERVE Transfer the chicken to individual plates and spoon the cooking liquid over the top. Serve right away with the lime wedges.

Chicken Tikka Masala

Although chicken tikka is traditionally cooked in a tandoor, I have adapted it for the slow cooker with excellent results. Because you put together the spice mixture and marinate the chicken the night before, you have little work the next day except for turning on the slow cooker. If you prefer some spicy heat, add ½–1 teaspoon cayenne pepper to the spice mixture. Serve with warmed naan bread or steamed basmati rice.

ingredients

5 cloves garlic, minced

1 heaping tablespoon peeled and grated fresh ginger

1 tablespoon ground cumin

1 tablespoon sweet paprika

2 teaspoons ground coriander

2 teaspoons garam masala

Kosher salt

1½ cups (12 oz/375 g) plain whole-milk yogurt (not Greek)

Juice of 1 lemon

4 lb (2 kg) skinless, bone-in chicken breast halves (4–5 breast halves)

2 tablespoons unsalted butter or ghee

1 yellow onion, finely chopped

1 can (28 oz/875 g) crushed tomatoes with juice

2 tablespoons tomato paste

2 teaspoons sugar (optional)

1 cup (8 fl oz/250 ml) heavy cream

Handful of fresh cilantro leaves, chopped

makes 8 servings

step by step

PREP In a small bowl, stir together the garlic, ginger, cumin, paprika, coriander, garam masala, and 1 tablespoon kosher salt. Then, in a second small bowl, combine the yogurt, lemon juice, and half of the spice mixture and stir to combine. Put the chicken in a large zippered plastic bag, pour in the yogurt mixture, and seal the bag closed. Turn the bag several times to coat the chicken evenly with the marinade. Tightly cover the remaining spice mixture, then refrigerate the chicken and the spice mixture overnight.

QUICK COOK Put the slow-cooker insert on the stove top over medium heat, then add the butter and warm to melt. Add the onion and cook, stirring, until it begins to turn translucent, about 5 minutes. Add the reserved spice mixture and cook, stirring, until fragrant, about 1 minute. Add the tomatoes, tomato paste, and the sugar, if using, and stir to scrape up any browned bits on the insert bottom.

SLOW COOK Transfer the insert to the slow cooker. Remove the chicken from the marinade and discard the marinade. Add the chicken to the slow cooker in a single layer, if possible, then turn the chicken to coat evenly with the sauce. Cover and cook on the low-heat setting for 4 hours. The chicken should be very tender and opaque throughout.

ASSEMBLE Transfer the chicken to a cutting board and let cool just until it can be handled. Meanwhile, stir the cream into the sauce in the slow cooker. Then, if you like, process the sauce with an immersion blender until smooth. Bone the chicken and discard the bones and any fat or gristle. Using your fingers or 2 forks, shred the meat into large chunks. Return the chicken to the slow cooker, stir well, re-cover, and cook on the low-heat setting for 30 minutes to warm the chicken through.

SERVE Transfer the chicken and sauce to a warm serving bowl or individual plates and garnish with the cilantro. Serve right away.

Burmese-Style Noodles
with
Chicken and Coconut

I first ate this noodle dish at Yamo's, a hole-in-the-wall restaurant in San Francisco with a cultlike following, and I have always wanted to re-create it at home. Using a slow cooker proved the perfect way to recapture those memorable flavors. For an authentic touch, top each serving with slices of hard-boiled egg and chopped green onion.

ingredients

2½ lb (1.25 kg) bone-in chicken thighs, skinned (about 6 large thighs)

Kosher salt

1 large yellow onion, halved and thinly sliced, plus ½ yellow onion, chopped

2 heaping tablespoons peeled and chopped fresh ginger

2 cloves garlic, chopped

2 cups (16 fl oz/500 ml) low-sodium chicken broth

1 tablespoon canola oil

3 tablespoons all-purpose flour

1 teaspoon ground turmeric

1 tablespoon sweet paprika

¼ teaspoon cayenne pepper (optional)

1 can (13½ fl oz/420 ml) coconut milk, shaken well before opening

Juice of 1 lime, plus lime wedges, for serving

¾ lb (375 g) fresh Chinese wheat noodles or spaghetti

Finely grated lime zest, optional

makes 6 servings

step by step

PREP Season the chicken with salt. In a blender, combine the chopped onion, the ginger, the garlic, and ½ cup (4 fl oz/125 ml) of the broth and process until puréed.

QUICK COOK Put the slow-cooker on the stove top over medium-high heat, then add the oil and warm until hot. Add the sliced onion and a pinch of salt and cook, stirring, until well browned, about 7 minutes. Stir in the flour and cook, stirring, until fully incorporated with the onion, about 30 seconds. Stir in the turmeric, paprika, and cayenne (if using), mixing well. Slowly pour in the remaining 1½ cups (12 fl oz/375 ml) broth while stirring constantly. Then add the onion purée and ½ teaspoon salt and mix well.

SLOW COOK Transfer the insert to the slow cooker, add the chicken, and turn the pieces to coat with the broth mixture. Cover and cook on the low-heat setting for 4 hours. The chicken should be very tender and opaque throughout.

ASSEMBLE Transfer the chicken to a cutting board. When just cool enough to handle, bone the chicken and discard the bones and any fat or gristle. Shred the meat into bite-size chunks with your fingers or 2 forks. Return the chicken to the slow cooker, add the coconut milk and lime juice, and stir to mix well. Re-cover and continue to cook on the low-heat setting for 30 minutes to warm the chicken and the sauce through.

While the chicken and sauce are reheating, prepare the noodles according to the package directions.

SERVE Put the noodles in a large bowl, add the chicken and sauce, and stir together to mix well. If desired, sprinkle with finely grated lime zest. Serve right away. Pass lime wedges at the table.

Teriyaki Chicken Thighs

Here's my take on teriyaki chicken, modified for the slow cooker. It is first marinated in a heady blend of garlic, ginger, soy sauce, and sesame oil and then slowly braised in mirin in the slow cooker, instead of being grilled. Serve these flavorful chicken thighs with steamed rice and stir-fried sugar snap peas.

ingredients

3–3½ lb (1.5–1.75 kg) bone-in chicken thighs, skinned (about 8 thighs)

Kosher salt and freshly ground pepper

1 clove garlic, minced

2-inch (5-cm) piece fresh ginger, peeled and finely chopped

½ cup (4 fl oz/125 ml) low-sodium soy sauce

1 teaspoon Asian sesame oil

1 tablespoon sugar

¼ cup (2 fl oz/60 ml) mirin

2 tablespoons unsalted butter, if including the optional browning step

2 tablespoons canola oil, if including the optional browning step

Sliced green onions, white and pale green parts, for garnish

makes 6–8 servings

step by step

PREP Season the chicken generously with salt and pepper. In a nonreactive bowl, stir together the garlic, ginger, soy sauce, and sesame oil. Add the chicken thighs and turn to coat evenly. Cover and marinate in the refrigerator, turning the chicken often, for at least 1 hour or up to overnight.

Remove the chicken from the marinade and discard the marinade. Pat the chicken dry with paper towels. In a small bowl, stir together the sugar and mirin until the sugar dissolves.

BUILD FLAVOR (OPTIONAL) Put the slow-cooker insert on the stove top over medium-high heat, then add the butter and oil and warm until hot. Working in batches to avoid crowding, add the chicken and cook, turning frequently, until browned, about 5 minutes. Return the browned chicken to the insert.

SLOW COOK If you have included the browning step, transfer the insert to the slow cooker, pour the mirin mixture over the chicken, and turn the thighs a few times to coat evenly. If you are starting here, put the marinated chicken in the slow cooker, pour in the mirin mixture, and turn the thighs a few times to coat evenly. Cover and cook on the low-heat setting for 5½ hours. The chicken should be tender and opaque throughout.

Uncover and cook on the high-heat setting, turning the chicken often, until most of the liquid has evaporated and the thighs are glazed, about 20 minutes longer.

SERVE Transfer the chicken to a platter, garnish with the green onions, and serve right away.

Italian-Style Chicken Stew

This dish makes me think of a typical Sunday supper prepared by a sweet Italian grandmother. The ingredients are simple, but after simmering together for hours in the slow cooker, they create a hearty, comforting dish that everyone in the family will love. Serve with hunks of hot crusty bread.

ingredients

Large pinch of saffron threads

⅓ cup (3 fl oz/80 ml) plus 3 tablespoons dry white wine

1 whole chicken, 4–5 lb (2–2.5 kg), cut into 10 pieces (2 thighs, 2 drumsticks, 2 wings, 4 breast portions), trimmed of excess skin and fat

¾ cup (4 oz/125 g) flour

Salt and freshly ground pepper

1 tablespoon olive oil

1 yellow onion, finely chopped

1 stalk celery, finely chopped

10 cloves garlic, smashed

¾ cup (6 fl oz/180 ml) low-sodium chicken broth

1 can (28 oz/875 g) diced tomatoes, drained

3 bay leaves

1½ teaspoons red wine vinegar

2 teaspoons finely chopped fresh flat-leaf parsley

makes 6 servings

step by step

PREP Soak the saffron in the 3 tablespoons wine for about 20 minutes. Meanwhile, pat the chicken pieces dry. In a plastic bag, combine the flour, ¾ teaspoon salt, and several grinds of pepper. One at a time, add the chicken pieces and toss to coat evenly. Remove the chicken from the bag, tapping off the excess flour.

BUILD FLAVOR Put the slow cooker insert on the stove top over medium-high heat, then add the oil and warm until hot. Working in batches to avoid crowding, add the chicken and cook, turning as needed, until golden brown on all sides, about 8 minutes total. Transfer the chicken to a plate.

QUICK COOK Pour off most of the fat from the insert and return it to medium heat. Add the onion and celery and sauté until softened and lightly golden, about 5 minutes. Add the garlic and cook for 1 minute. Pour in the remaining ⅓ cup wine and the stock and deglaze the insert, stirring and scraping up the browned bits on the insert bottom with a wooden spoon. Bring to a rapid simmer and cook to reduce slightly, about 10 minutes. Stir in the tomatoes, the saffron mixture, and the bay leaves.

SLOW COOK Transfer the insert to the slow cooker. Stack the chicken on top of the tomato mixture. Cover and cook on the low setting for 5–6 hours. The chicken should be tender and opaque throughout.

ASSEMBLE Transfer the chicken to a plate and keep warm. Remove and discard the bay leaves and stir the vinegar into the cooking liquid. Let stand for a few minutes, then skim away the fat from the surface with a large spoon.

SERVE Divide the chicken evenly among shallow bowls and ladle some of the braising liquid and vegetables over each portion. Sprinkle with parsley and serve right away.

Braised Chicken
with
Fennel, Orange, and Olives

For this dish, I was inspired by the classic Sicilian ingredients of fennel, orange, and black olives, and I use them to flavor tender chicken thighs. It's a simple dish, but impressive enough to serve at a dinner party. Serve roasted potatoes alongside and purchased orange sorbet for dessert.

ingredients

1 large orange

1 cup (8 fl oz/250 ml) low-sodium chicken broth

2 tablespoons whole-grain mustard

Kosher salt

6 large bone-in chicken thighs, skinned, about 2½ lb (1.25 kg) total weight

2 tablespoons unsalted butter

1 tablespoon canola oil

2 small fennel bulbs, about 1½ lb (750 g) total weight, stalks and fronds removed and bulbs cut lengthwise into thin wedges

⅓ cup (2 oz/60 g) coarsely chopped pitted Kalamata or Niçoise olives

makes 4–6 servings

step by step

PREP Zest and juice the orange, then strain the juice through a fine-mesh sieve into a small bowl. You should have about ½ cup (4 fl oz/125 ml). Add the zest, broth, mustard, and 1 teaspoon salt to the juice and whisk to combine. Season the chicken with 2 teaspoons salt.

BUILD FLAVOR Put the slow-cooker insert on the stove top over medium-high heat, then add the butter and oil and warm until hot. Working in batches to avoid crowding, add the chicken, bone side up, and cook until nicely browned on the underside, about 5 minutes. Transfer to a plate.

SLOW COOK Transfer the insert to the slow cooker, add the fennel and orange juice mixture, and toss and stir to mix well. Nestle the chicken pieces, bone side down, in the fennel mixture. Scatter the olives over the chicken. Cover and cook on the low-heat setting for 4½ hours. The chicken and fennel should be very tender and the chicken should be opaque throughout.

ASSEMBLE Transfer the chicken to a platter and cover to keep warm. Using a large spoon, skim off and discard as much fat as possible from the surface of the cooking liquid.

SERVE Transfer the chicken and fennel to individual plates and spoon the cooking liquid over the top. Serve right away.

Balsamic Chicken and Shallots

Red wine and balsamic vinegar provide an acidic touch that marries well with the sweetness of the shallots. Don't be put off by the amount of shallots used here. As they cook, their potency diminishes and their natural sweetness emerges. Serve the chicken with mashed potatoes and roasted broccoli.

ingredients

2 lb (1 kg) shallots, peeled

1 chicken, 4–5 lb (2–2.5 kg), cut into 8 serving pieces, trimmed of excess skin and fat

Kosher salt and freshly ground pepper

1 tablespoon unsalted butter

1 tablespoon canola oil

¼ cup (2 fl oz/60 ml) dry red wine

½ cup (4 fl oz/125 ml) low-sodium chicken broth

¼ cup (2 fl oz/60 ml) balsamic vinegar

makes 4–6 servings

step by step

PREP Peel the shallots, then, using a paring knife, cut a shallow X in the root end of each shallot. Set aside. Season the chicken pieces with salt and pepper.

BUILD FLAVOR (OPTIONAL) Put the slow-cooker insert on the stove top over medium-high heat, then add the butter and oil and warm until hot. Working in batches if necessary to avoid crowding, add the chicken pieces and cook, turning frequently, until browned, about 10 minutes. Transfer to a plate and set aside.

QUICK COOK If you have included the browning step, pour off all but 2 tablespoons of the fat from the insert and return the insert to medium-high heat. If you are starting here, put the slow-cooker insert on the stove top over medium-high heat, then add the butter and oil and warm until hot. Add the shallots and sauté until lightly browned, about 5 minutes. Add the wine, broth, and vinegar, raise the heat to high, and deglaze the insert, stirring and scraping up the browned bits on the insert bottom with a wooden spoon. Bring to a boil.

SLOW COOK Transfer the insert to the slow cooker, add the chicken, and stir and turn the pieces to coat evenly with the shallot mixture. Cover and cook on the low-heat setting for 6 hours. The chicken should be tender and opaque throughout.

ASSEMBLE Transfer the chicken and shallots to a bowl or plate and cover to keep warm. Bring the liquid to a simmer on the high-heat setting and cook, uncovered, until slightly thickened, about 10 minutes. Season with salt and pepper.

SERVE Arrange the chicken and shallots on a platter and spoon the cooking liquid over the top. Serve right away.

Chicken and Andouille Gumbo

A good gumbo takes many hours to build its signature flavor, which means the slow cooker is a perfect medium for preparing it. Fresh okra is added to the spicy stew near the end of the cooking so that it doesn't get too gummy. Stay with tradition and serve the gumbo with a side of steamed rice and set out a bottle of hot-pepper sauce.

ingredients

1 chicken, 4–5 lb (2–2.5 kg) cut into 8 serving pieces, trimmed of excess skin and fat

Kosher salt and freshly ground black pepper

2 tablespoons unsalted butter

2 tablespoons canola oil, plus ⅓ cup (3 fl oz/80 ml)

1 yellow onion, finely chopped

1 small, green bell pepper, seeded and chopped

1 small red bell pepper, seeded and chopped

1 rib celery, chopped

2 cloves garlic, minced

⅓ cup (2 oz/60 g) all-purpose flour

3 cups (24 fl oz/750 ml) low-sodium chicken broth

¾ lb (375 g) andouille sausage, cut into ½-inch (12-mm) pieces

1 lb (500 g) okra, trimmed and cut into slices ½ inch (12 mm) thick

¼ teaspoon cayenne pepper

makes 4–6 servings

step by step

PREP Season the chicken with the salt and black pepper.

BUILD FLAVOR (OPTIONAL) Put the slow cooker insert on the stove top over medium-high heat, then add the butter and the 2 tablespoons oil and warm until hot. Working in batches to avoid crowding, add the chicken and cook, turning frequently, until browned, about 10 minutes. Transfer to a large plate and set aside.

QUICK COOK If you have included the browning step, pour off all but 1 tablespoon of the fat from the insert. If you are starting from here, put the slow cooker insert on the stove top over medium-high heat, then add the butter and the 2 tablespoons oil and warm until hot. Add the onion, bell peppers, and celery and sauté over medium-high heat until softened, about 5 minutes. Add the garlic and cook for 1 minute longer. Scrape onto the plate with the chicken.

In the insert, on the stove top over medium-high heat, warm the ⅓ cup (3 fl oz/80 ml) oil. Add the flour and cook, whisking frequently, until the mixture turns light brown, about 5 minutes. Add the broth, raise the heat to high, bring to a boil, and cook, whisking constantly, until thickened, 5–7 minutes.

SLOW COOK Pour the broth mixture into the insert. Add the chicken and vegetables, then add the sausage. Cover and cook for 6 hours on the low-heat setting. The chicken should be tender and opaque throughout.

Uncover and use a large, shallow spoon or a ladle to skim off as much fat as possible from the surface of the cooking liquid. Add the okra, cover, and cook until tender, about 30 minutes longer.

SERVE Stir in the cayenne and season to taste with salt and black pepper. Divide the gumbo among bowls and serve right away.

Coq au Vin Blanc

The classic version of coq au vin directs you to cook and layer almost every ingredient separately. I have traded out those time-consuming directions and the typical red wine in favor of this quick and easy version using white wine that calls for sautéing most of the ingredients together, then combining them with the browned chicken and leaving everything to simmer in the slow cooker. Browning the chicken here is recommended, as it noticeably boosts the flavor. Serve this dish over buttered egg noodles.

ingredients

3 tablespoons all-purpose flour

Kosher salt and freshly ground pepper

2½ lb (1.25 kg) skinless, bone-in chicken thighs (about 6 large thighs)

2 slices thick-cut bacon, chopped

½ large yellow onion, finely chopped

2 tablespoons unsalted butter

1 lb (500 g) small cremini mushrooms, brushed clean and left whole if very small or halved if large

2 carrots, peeled and finely chopped

1¼ cups (10 fl oz/310 ml) dry white wine (I like dry Riesling)

¾ cup (6 fl oz/180 ml) low-sodium chicken broth

1 large sprig fresh thyme

makes 6 servings

step by step

PREP On a plate, stir together the flour, 2 teaspoons salt, and several grinds of pepper. Turn the chicken pieces in the seasoned flour, coating evenly and shaking off any excess.

BUILD FLAVOR Put the slow-cooker insert on the stove top over medium-high heat, then add the bacon and fry until the fat has rendered and the bacon is crisp, about 5 minutes. Add the onion and cook, stirring and scraping up any browned bits from the insert bottom with a wooden spoon, until the onion is slightly softened, about 2 minutes. Transfer to a small bowl and set aside.

Return the insert to medium-high heat, then add the butter and warm until melted. Working in batches to avoid crowding, add the chicken, bone side up, and cook until nicely browned on the underside, about 5 minutes. Transfer to a plate and set aside.

SLOW COOK Transfer the insert to the slow cooker, add the mushrooms, carrots, wine, broth, thyme, and the reserved bacon and onion, and stir well. Nestle the chicken, bone side down, in a single layer in the broth mixture. Cover and cook on the low-heat setting for 4 hours. The chicken should be very tender and opaque throughout.

SERVE Remove and discard the thyme. Transfer the chicken and sauce to individual shallow bowls and serve right away.

Chicken in Green Mole

Mexican moles are beautifully complex and can take hours—sometimes days—to prepare. But don't let that discourage you; in this streamlined version, featuring pumpkin seeds and tangy tomatillos, the slow cooker does most of the work for you.

ingredients

¼ cup (2 fl oz/60 ml) olive oil

1 white onion, chopped

2 cloves garlic, chopped

3 jalapeño chiles, seeded and coarsely chopped

1½ cups shelled pumpkin seeds (pepitas)

1½ cups (12 fl oz/375 ml) low-sodium chicken broth

¾ lb (375 g) tomatillos, husks removed and coarsely chopped

¾ cup loosely packed fresh cilantro leaves, plus more for garnish

1 teaspoon dried oregano

Kosher salt

3 lb (1.5 kg) skinless, boneless chicken thighs (about 8 thighs)

¼ cup (2 fl oz/60 ml) sour cream

makes 6—8 servings

step by step

PREP In a large frying pan over medium-high heat, warm the oil. Add the onion and sauté until it starts to turn tender, about 3 minutes. Stir in the garlic and chiles and sauté for about 30 seconds. Add the pumpkin seeds and cook, stirring, until they darken in color, about 5 minutes. Stir in the broth, tomatillos, cilantro, oregano, and 1 teaspoon salt, and bring to a boil.

Ladle about half of the pumpkin seed mixture into a blender or food processor and pulse a few times. Add the remaining mixture and blend or process until it forms a uniformly coarse purée.

SLOW COOK Transfer the purée to the slow cooker. Add the chicken thighs. Cover and cook for 6 hours on the low-heat setting. The chicken should be tender and opaque throughout.

SERVE Divide the chicken among plates. Spoon the sauce over the chicken. Garnish with cilantro leaves and the sour cream and serve right away.

Mediterranean Chicken Stew

Inspired by the flavors of southern France and Italy, this aromatic stew brings
together garlic, olives, tomatoes, and full-bodied red wine. Serve this over buttered
egg noodles or Israeli couscous and set out a tossed green salad, if you like.

ingredients

3 lb (1.5 kg) chicken drumsticks and
thighs (12 pieces total)

Kosher salt and freshly ground pepper

2 cups (16 fl oz/500 ml) full-bodied
red wine

2 shallots, minced

3 cloves garlic, minced

6 peppercorns

3 or 4 sprigs fresh thyme

3 tomatoes, seeded and chopped

1 tablespoon tomato paste

1 tablespoon unsalted butter,
cut into small pieces

1 tablespoon all-purpose flour

1 cup (4 oz/125 g) brined black or green
olives, pitted and coarsely chopped

makes 6–8 servings

step by step

PREP Season the chicken with salt and pepper.

QUICK COOK Put the slow-cooker insert on the stove top over high
heat and add the wine, shallots, garlic, peppercorns, and thyme. Bring
to a boil and cook, stirring frequently, until reduced to about ½ cup
(4 fl oz/125 ml), about 20 minutes.

SLOW COOK Transfer the insert to the slow cooker, add the chicken
and tomatoes, and mix evenly with the wine mixture. Cover and cook
on the low-heat setting for 6 hours. The chicken should be tender and
opaque throughout.

ASSEMBLE Transfer the chicken to a platter and cover to keep warm.
Strain the cooking liquid through a fine-mesh sieve into a small bowl.
You should have about 1 cup (8 fl oz/250 ml). Whisk in the tomato paste.
Put the insert on the stove top over medium-high heat. Add the butter.
When the butter melts, whisk in the flour. Slowly add the tomato paste–
cooking liquid mixture and bring the liquid to a boil. Cook, whisking
constantly, until a thick sauce forms, 7–10 minutes. Stir in the olives and
season with salt and pepper. Add the chicken, turn to coat with the sauce,
and cook over medium-low heat until warmed through, about 5 minutes.

SERVE Transfer the chicken to individual plates, spoon the sauce over
the top, and serve right away.

Chicken Cacciatore

Cacciatore, which means "hunter" in Italian, is a rustic country dish most often made with chicken, but also sometimes with rabbit. This version is full of meaty mushrooms—as a hunter might find in the woods—and tomatoes. Serve it with crusty bread or over freshly cooked pasta.

ingredients

1 chicken, 4–5 lb (2–2.5 kg), cut into 8 serving pieces, trimmed of excess skin and fat

Kosher salt and freshly ground pepper

3 tablespoons olive oil

1 tablespoon fresh lemon juice

1 clove garlic, minced

1 tablespoon chopped fresh thyme

2 tablespoons unsalted butter

1 yellow onion, thinly sliced

½ lb (250 g) cremini mushrooms, brushed clean and halved or quartered if large

1 can (28 oz/875 g) whole plum tomatoes with juice, lightly crushed with your hands

2 tablespoons capers, rinsed

1 teaspoon anchovy paste (optional)

¼ cup (2 fl oz/60 ml) low-sodium chicken broth

makes 6–8 servings

step by step

PREP Season the chicken with salt and pepper. In a nonreactive bowl, stir together 2 tablespoons of the oil, the lemon juice, garlic, and thyme. Add the chicken pieces and turn to coat. Cover and marinate in the refrigerator, turning the chicken pieces occasionally, for at least 1 hour or up to overnight.

BUILD FLAVOR (OPTIONAL) Remove the chicken from the marinade and pat dry with paper towels; discard the marinade. Put the slow-cooker insert on the stove top over medium-high heat, then add the butter and the remaining 1 tablespoon oil and warm until hot. Working in batches to avoid crowding, add the chicken pieces and cook, turning frequently, until browned, about 10 minutes. Transfer to a plate and set aside.

QUICK COOK If you have included the browning step, pour off all but 1 tablespoon of the fat from the insert and return the insert to medium-high heat. If you are starting here, put the slow-cooker insert on the stove top over medium-high heat, then add the butter and the remaining 1 tablespoon oil and warm until hot. Add the onion and cook, stirring, until softened, 3–5 minutes. Add the mushrooms and cook, stirring, until they begin to soften, 6–8 minutes. Stir in the tomatoes, capers, anchovy paste (if using), and broth. Raise the heat to high and deglaze the insert, stirring and scraping up the browned bits on the insert bottom with a wooden spoon. Bring to a boil.

SLOW COOK Transfer the insert to the slow cooker and add the chicken. Cover and cook on the low-heat setting for 6 hours. The chicken should be tender and opaque throughout.

ASSEMBLE Transfer the chicken to a platter and tent with aluminum foil to keep warm. Using a large spoon, skim off and discard as much fat as possible from the surface of the cooking liquid. Bring the liquid to a simmer on the high-heat setting and cook, uncovered, until reduced and thickened, 5–10 minutes. Season with salt and pepper.

SERVE Spoon the cooking liquid over the chicken and serve right away.

Chicken Tagine
with
Olives and Lemon

This colorful Moroccan-inspired stew offers a tantalizing combination of spicy, sweet, salty, and tangy flavors. Lemon juice and lemon zest stand in for the typical preserved lemons of the region, making it easy to achieve on a busy night. Serve this full-flavored dish over a mound of Israeli or regular couscous or buttered orzo.

ingredients

3 tablespoons all-purpose flour

Kosher salt and freshly ground pepper

3½ lb (1.75 kg) bone-in chicken breasts and thighs, skinned

⅛ teaspoon saffron threads

1½ cups (12 fl oz/375 ml) low-sodium chicken broth

3 tablespoons olive oil

1 yellow onion, finely chopped

4 cloves garlic, minced

2 teaspoons hot paprika

1 teaspoon ground cumin

1 teaspoon ground ginger

½ teaspoon ground cinnamon

½ teaspoon ground coriander

2 cups (10 oz/315 g) pitted green olives, coarsely chopped

¼ cup (2 fl oz/60 ml) fresh lemon juice

2 tablespoons grated lemon zest

3 tablespoons finely chopped fresh mint

makes 6—8 servings

step by step

PREP On a plate, stir together the flour, 1 teaspoon salt, and ½ teaspoon pepper. Turn the chicken pieces in the seasoned flour, coating evenly and shaking off any excess. In a small bowl, crumble the saffron into the broth.

BUILD FLAVOR (OPTIONAL) Put the slow-cooker insert on the stove top over medium-high heat, then add the oil and warm until hot. Working in batches to avoid crowding, add the chicken pieces and cook, turning as needed, until golden brown, about 10 minutes. Transfer to a plate and set aside.

QUICK COOK If you have included the browning step, pour off all but 3 tablespoons of the fat from the insert and return the insert to medium-high heat. If you are starting here, put the slow-cooker insert on the stove top over medium-high heat, then add the oil and warm until hot. Add the onion and garlic and cook, stirring, just until fragrant, about 30 seconds. Add the paprika, cumin, ginger, cinnamon, and coriander and cook, stirring, until the spices are fragrant and evenly coat the onion-garlic mixture, about 1 minute. Pour in the broth-saffron mixture and deglaze the insert, stirring and scraping up the browned bits on the insert bottom with a wooden spoon. Bring to a boil.

SLOW COOK Transfer the insert to the slow cooker and add the chicken, arranging the thighs on the bottom and the breasts on top. Cover and cook on the low-heat setting for 5—6 hours.

About 1 hour before the chicken is done, uncover and scatter the olives over the chicken, then sprinkle with the lemon juice and zest. Re-cover and continue to cook on the low-heat setting until the chicken is tender and opaque throughout.

SERVE Transfer the chicken to plates, spoon the cooking juices and olives over the top, and garnish with the mint. Serve right away.

Spicy Chicken Tostadas

The sauce for this Latin-inspired dish comes together in 10 minutes or less and is packed with fiery flavor. I love this shredded, spicy chicken on tostadas, but it can also be used to make tacos or burritos or in a salad with lettuce, cherry tomatoes, diced avocado, black beans, and lime vinaigrette.

ingredients

3 lb (1.5 kg) bone-in chicken thighs, skinned (about 8 large thighs)

Kosher salt

1 tablespoon canola oil

1 large yellow onion, halved and sliced

5 cloves garlic, chopped

1 can (15 oz/470 g) diced fire-roasted tomatoes with juice

1 can (7 oz/220 g) chipotle chiles in adobo sauce, seeded if you like less spice

Juice of 1 lime

Crema or sour cream, queso fresco or feta cheese, sliced avocado, fresh cilantro leaves, shredded cabbage or lettuce, and lime wedges for serving

12 flat corn tostada shells, about 6 inches (15 cm) in diameter

makes 6—8 servings

step by step

PREP Season the chicken with salt.

QUICK COOK Put the slow-cooker insert on the stove top over medium-high heat, then add the oil and warm until hot. Add the onion and cook, stirring, until golden, about 6 minutes. Add the garlic and cook, stirring, until fragrant, about 1 minute.

Transfer the onion and garlic to a blender and add the tomatoes with their juice, the chipotle chiles and adobo sauce, and the lime juice and process to a smooth purée.

SLOW COOK Transfer the insert to the slow cooker and add the chicken. Pour the puréed sauce over the chicken thighs and turn them to coat evenly. Cover and cook on the low-heat setting for 4 hours. The chicken should be very tender and opaque throughout.

ASSEMBLE Transfer the chicken to a cutting board. When just cool enough to handle, bone the chicken and discard the bones and any fat or gristle. Using your fingers or 2 forks, shred the meat into small bite-size pieces. Transfer the meat to a serving bowl and add enough sauce (about half) to coat the chicken, turning the chicken in the sauce. (Let the remaining sauce cool, then transfer to an airtight container and refrigerate for up to 3 days or freeze for up to 3 months. Toss it with noodles or drizzle over roasted pork or grilled steak or chicken.)

SERVE Put the crema, queso fresco, avocado, cilantro, cabbage, and lime wedges in separate bowls and set on the table to use as toppings. Spoon some of the chicken and sauce onto each tostada shell, then invite diners to top them as desired.

Red Curry Chicken and Eggplant

Thai curries pack loads of layered flavors. Here, delicate eggplant and aromatic Thai basil join tender chicken thighs in a light, fragrant sauce infused with creamy coconut milk. Serve with plenty of warm jasmine rice.

ingredients

½ yellow onion, coarsely chopped

6 cloves garlic

3 tablespoons Thai red curry paste

Grated zest and juice of 2 limes

2 tablespoons Asian fish sauce

2 tablespoons packed golden brown sugar

Kosher salt

1 cup (8 fl oz/250 ml) low-sodium chicken broth

1 can (13½ fl oz/440 ml) coconut milk, shaken well before opening

3 lb (1.5 kg) bone-in chicken thighs, skinned (about 8 thighs)

1 lb (500 g) Japanese or Asian eggplants (about 3 eggplants), trimmed, halved lengthwise, and sliced

½ cup (¾ oz/20 g) coarsely chopped fresh basil, preferably Thai basil

¼ cup (1 oz/30 g) unsweetened shredded dried coconut, toasted (optional)

makes 6—8 servings

step by step

PREP In a food processor, combine the onion, garlic, curry paste, lime zest and juice, fish sauce, brown sugar, and ¼ teaspoon salt. Pulse until a chunky purée forms. Pour into the slow cooker, then stir in the broth and coconut milk.

SLOW COOK Season the chicken thighs with salt and add them to the insert, turning to coat them with the red curry mixture. Cover and cook on the low setting for 4 hours.

Uncover, add the eggplant, re-cover, and continue to cook for another 1—2 hours, or until the eggplant and chicken are very tender and the chicken is opaque throughout.

ASSEMBLE Uncover, and, using a slotted spoon, transfer the chicken pieces to a plate. Remove the meat from the bones, and discard the bones and any fat or gristle. Chop or shred the meat. Return the chicken meat to the slow cooker and stir. Re-cover and continue to cook on the low-heat setting for 30 minutes to warm through.

SERVE Stir the basil into the curry, then transfer the curry to a large serving bowl. Garnish with the toasted coconut, if using, and serve right away.

Chicken-Tortilla Soup

This colorful soup, full of vibrant Latin spices and a multitude of textures, is one of my family's favorite dishes. It's also a great option for a festive gathering. Put out bowls of toppings and let each diner personalize their own serving to their liking.

ingredients

1 can (15 oz/470 g) crushed tomatoes

1 yellow onion, coarsely chopped

3 cloves garlic, smashed

1 jalapeño chile, seeded and chopped

5 cups (40 fl oz/1.25 l) low-sodium chicken broth

2½ lb (1.25 kg) bone-in chicken thighs (about 6 thighs), skinned, trimmed of excess fat

Juice of 1 lime

1 teaspoon red wine vinegar

1 teaspoon ground cumin

3 bay leaves

Kosher salt and freshly ground pepper

2½ cups corn kernels, thawed if frozen

Diced avocado, crumbled queso fresco or feta cheese, chopped fresh cilantro, tortilla chips, and lime wedges for serving

makes 6 servings

step by step

PREP In a blender or food processor, combine the tomatoes, onion, garlic, chile, and 1 cup (8 fl oz/250 ml) of the stock and process until smooth. Pour into a slow cooker insert.

SLOW COOK Add the chicken thighs, the remaining 4 cups (32 fl oz/1 l) broth, the lime juice, vinegar, cumin, bay leaves, ¾ teaspoon salt, and several grinds of pepper. Cover and cook on the low setting for 5 hours. The chicken should be tender and opaque throughout.

ASSEMBLE Transfer the chicken pieces to a plate. Remove the meat from the bones, and discard the bones and any fat or gristle. Chop or shred the meat. Using a large spoon, skim away the fat from the braising liquid. Return the chicken meat to the slow cooker. Add the corn kernels, cover, and cook on the low-heat setting until tender, about 15 minutes more.

SERVE Remove and discard the bay leaves. Ladle the soup into shallow bowls, distributing the ingredients evenly. Put the avocado, queso fresco, cilantro, chips, and lime wedges in separate bowls and set on the table for diners to help themselves.

Pulled Chicken Tacos

Simple and versatile, this spicy pulled chicken is delicious in tacos but can also be combined with shredded jack cheese in quesadillas, tossed into a simple green salad, or spooned onto a toasted bun and doused with barbecue sauce.

ingredients

1 tablespoon chili powder

1 teaspoon ground cumin

Kosher salt

2½ lb (1.25 kg) bone-in chicken thighs, skinned (about 6 large thighs)

Grated zest and juice of 1 lime, plus more juice if needed

½ cup (4 fl oz/125 ml) low-sodium chicken broth

Shredded lettuce, chopped tomatoes, salsa, sour cream or plain yogurt, and shredded Monterey jack or Cheddar cheese for serving

12–18 corn tortillas, 6 inches (15 cm) in diameter, warmed

makes 6 servings

step by step

PREP In a small bowl, stir together the chili powder, cumin, and 1 teaspoon salt. Season the chicken with the spice mixture.

SLOW COOK Arrange the chicken thighs in a single layer in the slow cooker. Sprinkle evenly with the lime zest and lime juice, then pour in the broth. Cover and cook on the low-heat setting for 4 hours. The chicken should be very tender and opaque throughout.

ASSEMBLE Transfer the chicken to a cutting board. When just cool enough to handle, bone the chicken and discard the bones and any fat or gristle. Using your fingers or 2 forks, shred the meat into bite-size pieces. Transfer the meat to a serving bowl. Using a large spoon, skim off and discard the fat from the surface of the cooking liquid. Moisten the meat with some of the cooking liquid, then taste and season the meat with more lime juice and salt if needed.

SERVE Put the lettuce, tomatoes, salsa, sour cream, and cheese in separate bowls and place on the table along with the chicken and the tortillas and let diners make their own tacos.

Lemon-Olive Chicken

The foundation of this recipe consists of simple browned-then-braised chicken legs, which can be served a multitude of ways. Here, they are brightened with a tangy-salty relish made from lemons, olives, almonds, and herbs. Feel free to substitute chicken thighs for the legs, if you like.

ingredients

3 lb (1.5 kg) chicken drumsticks, trimmed of excess fat

Kosher salt and freshly ground pepper

4 tablespoons (2 fl oz/60 ml) olive oil

½ yellow onion, finely chopped

2 stalks celery, finely chopped

2 sprigs fresh thyme

3 bay leaves

5 cloves garlic, finely chopped

⅓ cup (3 fl oz/80 ml) dry white wine

¼ cup (2 fl oz/60 ml) low-sodium chicken broth

1 teaspoon white wine vinegar

1 small lemon

1¼ cups (7½ oz/235 g) green olives, pitted and roughly chopped

⅓ cup (2 oz/60 g) chopped blanched almonds

Large handful of fresh flat-leaf parsley leaves

makes 6 servings

step by step

PREP Season the chicken with salt and pepper.

BUILD FLAVOR (OPTIONAL) Put the slow cooker insert on the stove top over medium-high heat, then add 2 tablespoons of the oil and warm until hot. Working in batches to avoid crowding, add the chicken and cook, turning frequently, until browned, about 5 minutes. Transfer the chicken to a plate.

QUICK COOK If you have included the browning step, pour off most of the fat from the insert and return it to medium-high heat. If you are starting from here, put the slow cooker insert on the stove top over medium-high heat. Add 2 tablespoons of the oil and warm until hot. Add the onion, celery, thyme, and bay leaves and sauté until the vegetables are just beginning to color, about 5 minutes. Add the garlic and cook for 1 minute more. Pour in the wine, broth, and vinegar and deglaze, stirring and scraping up any browned bits on the pan bottom.

SLOW COOK Transfer the insert to a slow cooker and place the chicken on top. Cover and cook on the low setting for about 3 hours. The chicken should be tender and opaque throughout.

ASSEMBLE Transfer the chicken to a platter and cover to keep warm. Cut the lemon in half and remove the seeds. Roughly chop the lemon, then add to a food processor along with the olives, almonds, and parsley. Pulse a few times until it forms a coarse, even texture. Transfer to a bowl and stir in the remaining 2 tablespoons oil, a scant ¼ teaspoon salt, and a few grinds of pepper. Skim off the fat from the braising liquid in the slow cooker insert with a large spoon.

SERVE Drizzle some of the warm braising liquid over the chicken, top with the lemon-olive relish, and serve right away.

Buffalo-Style Chicken Legs

For this recipe, I took a favorite bar food and created a crave-worthy main dish by swapping chicken drumsticks for chicken wings and popping them in the slow cooker to simmer in their signature spicy sauce. Serve with a green salad with sliced celery and blue cheese dressing and warmed garlic bread.

ingredients

5 lb (2.5 kg) chicken drumsticks, trimmed of excess fat

Kosher salt and freshly ground pepper

1 tablespoon olive oil

½ yellow onion, finely chopped

2 stalks celery, finely chopped

10 cloves garlic, chopped

2 chipotle chiles in adobo sauce, chopped

6 tablespoons (3 oz/90 g) tomato paste

½ cup (4 fl oz/125 ml) beer

½ cup (4 fl oz/125 ml) medium-spicy hot sauce, such as Frank's

2 teaspoons rice vinegar

1 tablespoon firmly packed golden brown sugar

makes 8 servings

step by step

PREP Season the chicken with salt and pepper.

BUILD FLAVOR (OPTIONAL) Put the slow cooker insert on the stove top over medium-high heat, then add the oil and warm until hot. Working in batches to avoid crowding, add the chicken and cook, turning frequently, until browned, about 5 minutes. Transfer the chicken to a plate.

QUICK COOK If you have included the browning step, pour off some of the fat from the insert and return it to medium-high heat. If you are starting from here, put the slow cooker insert on the stove top over medium-high heat, then add the oil and warm until hot. Add the onion and celery and sauté until just beginning to brown, about 5 minutes. Add the garlic, chiles, and tomato paste and sauté for 2 minutes more. Pour in the beer, hot sauce, and vinegar and deglaze, stirring and scraping up any browned bits on the pan bottom.

SLOW COOK Transfer the insert to the slow cooker. Cover and cook on the low setting for about 5 hours. The chicken should be tender and opaque throughout.

ASSEMBLE Transfer the chicken to a plate. Using a large spoon, skim off the fat from the braising liquid. Transfer the liquid to a blender or food processor and process until smooth. Return to the insert, place over high heat, and stir in the brown sugar. Cook, stirring occasionally, until thickened, about 10 minutes. Return the drumsticks to the sauce and simmer until heated through, about 10 minutes.

SERVE Transfer the chicken to a platter and serve right away, passing additional sauce at the table.

Chicken and White Bean Chili

This variation on a traditional beef chili features tender braised chicken in
a cannellini bean and ale-spiked stew. To dress up the chili, top each serving
with a spoonful of guacamole or some diced avocado and a scattering
of shredded Monterey jack cheese and serve tortilla chips on the side.

ingredients

3 lb (1.5 kg) bone-in chicken thighs,
skinned (about 8 thighs)

Kosher salt and freshly ground
black pepper

1 tablespoon canola oil

2 green bell peppers, seeded and
finely chopped

1 yellow onion, finely chopped

1 small jalapeño chile, minced

2 teaspoons minced garlic

¼ cup (2 oz/60 g) tomato paste

3 tablespoons all-purpose flour

1 bottle (12 fl oz/375 ml) brown ale

3 cups (18 oz/560 g) canned crushed
fire-roasted tomatoes with juice

2 cups (16 fl oz/500 ml) low-sodium
chicken broth

¼ cup (2 fl oz/60 ml) fresh orange juice

1 tablespoon honey

1 teaspoon ground cumin

1 teaspoon dried oregano

½ teaspoon ground coriander

¼ teaspoon ground cinnamon

1 can (15 oz/470 g) white beans,
drained and rinsed

½ cup (¾ oz/20 g) finely chopped
fresh cilantro

makes 6 servings

step by step

PREP Season the chicken with ½ teaspoon salt and a few grinds of
black pepper.

QUICK COOK Put the slow-cooker insert on the stove top over medium-
high heat, then add the oil and warm until hot. Add the bell peppers, onion,
chile, and garlic and cook, stirring, until softened, about 5 minutes. Whisk
in the tomato paste and flour and cook, stirring, until the flour is fully
incorporated, about 30 seconds. Pour in the ale and simmer for 4 minutes.
Add the tomatoes, broth, orange juice, honey, cumin, oregano, coriander,
cinnamon, 1 teaspoon salt, and a few grinds pepper and bring to a boil.

SLOW COOK Transfer the insert to the slow cooker, add the beans, and
stir to combine. Add the chicken thighs, immersing them in the sauce.
Cover and cook on the low-heat setting for 4–5 hours. The chicken should
be tender and opaque throughout.

ASSEMBLE Transfer the chicken to a cutting board and let cool just
until it can be handled. Bone the chicken and discard the bones and any
fat or gristle. Using your fingers or 2 forks, shred the meat into small
bite-size pieces. Return the chicken to the insert, add the cilantro, and
stir well. Cover and cook on the low-heat setting for 30 minutes to
warm through.

SERVE Transfer the chili to individual bowls and serve right away.

Braised Chicken
with
White Wine and Herbs

This simple dish showcases the flavors of fresh herbs and white wine to breathe new life into a chicken dinner. Vary the side dishes with the seasons, offering sautéed seasonal vegetables and roasted potatoes as accompaniments.

ingredients

3 lb (1.5 kg) skin-on, bone-in chicken thighs (about 8 thighs)

Kosher salt and freshly ground pepper

2 tablespoons olive oil

½ yellow onion, finely chopped

4 cloves garlic, smashed

2 sprigs fresh thyme

2 sprigs fresh oregano

3 bay leaves

⅓ cup (3 fl oz/80 ml) dry white wine

2 teaspoons white wine vinegar

⅓ cup (3 fl oz/80 ml) low-sodium chicken broth

makes 6 servings

step by step

PREP Season the chicken with salt and pepper.

BUILD FLAVOR (OPTIONAL) Put the slow cooker insert on the stove top over medium-high heat, then add the oil and warm until hot. Working in batches to avoid crowding, add the chicken, skin side down, and cook until browned, about 4 minutes. Do not turn. Transfer the chicken to a plate and set aside.

QUICK COOK If you have included the browning step, keep the insert over medium heat. If you are starting from here, put the slow cooker insert on the stove top over medium-high heat, then add the oil and warm until hot. Add the onion, garlic, thyme, oregano, and bay leaves to the insert and sauté until the vegetables are just beginning to brown, about 5 minutes. Pour in the wine and vinegar and deglaze, stirring and scraping to dislodge any browned bits on the pan bottom. Stir in the broth, ½ teaspoon salt, and several grinds of pepper.

SLOW COOK Transfer the insert to the slow cooker. Add the chicken to the insert, submerging it in the liquid. Cover and cook on the low setting for 4 hours. The chicken should be tender and opaque throughout.

ASSEMBLE Transfer the chicken to a plate and keep warm. Remove and discard the bay leaves and the thyme and oregano sprigs. Let the braising liquid stand for a few minutes, then skim off the fat with a large spoon.

SERVE Divide the chicken thighs among warm individual plates. Drizzle with some of the braising liquid and serve right away.

Orange Chicken
with
Soy and Ginger

This surprisingly simple dish is packed with so much flavor that anyone you serve it to will think you spent hours putting it together. Serve it with fragrant jasmine rice and a tossed green salad with orange vinaigrette.

ingredients

1 chicken, 4–5 lb (2–2.5 kg), cut into 8 serving pieces, trimmed of excess skin and fat

4 strips orange zest, each about 3 inches (7.5 cm) long

2 star anise

2 cinnamon sticks, each 3 inches (7.5 cm) long

2-inch (5-cm) piece fresh ginger, peeled and thinly sliced

2 tablespoons firmly packed dark brown sugar

1¼ cups (10 fl oz/10 ml) low-sodium soy sauce

2 cups (16 fl oz/500 ml) low-sodium chicken broth

2 tablespoons Asian sesame oil

½ cup (4 fl oz/125 ml) dry sherry

2½ tablespoons cornstarch

makes 4–6 servings

step by step

SLOW COOK Place the chicken in the insert in the slow cooker. Scatter the orange zest, star anise, cinnamon, and ginger around the chicken and sprinkle evenly with the brown sugar. Pour in the soy sauce and 1 cup (8 fl oz/250 ml) of the broth. Cover and cook for 6 hours on the low-heat setting. The chicken should be tender and opaque throughout.

ASSEMBLE Transfer the chicken to a platter, brush with the sesame oil and cover loosely with aluminum foil to keep warm. Pour the cooking liquid into a saucepan and add the sherry. In a small cup, stir the cornstarch into the remaining 1 cup (8 fl oz/250 ml) broth until completely dissolved. Stir into the cooking liquid and cook over medium heat until the sauce thickens, about 5 minutes. Remove and discard the zest strips, star anise, cinnamon, and ginger.

SERVE Divide the chicken pieces and sauce among individual plates and serve right away.

Chicken Paprikash

The deep, rich color and slightly piquant flavor of paprika lays the groundwork for this classic Hungarian stew. There are many versions out there, but I like to make mine in the slow cooker. Seek out a good-quality Hungarian paprika for this dish and add a bit of hot paprika to the mix, if you like it spicy. Serve over hot cooked egg noodles.

ingredients

1 chicken, 4–5 lb (2–2.5 kg), cut into 8 serving pieces, trimmed of excess skin and fat

Kosher salt and freshly ground pepper

2 tablespoons unsalted butter, if including the optional browning step

2 tablespoons canola oil

2 yellow onions, finely chopped

1 green bell pepper, seeded and finely chopped

½ cup (4 fl oz/125 ml) low-sodium chicken broth

2 tablespoons sweet paprika

1 teaspoon hot paprika (optional)

2 tomatoes, seeded and chopped

½ cup (4 oz/125 g) sour cream

makes 4–6 servings

step by step

PREP Season the chicken with salt and pepper.

BUILD FLAVOR (OPTIONAL) Put the slow-cooker insert on the stove top over medium-high heat, then add the butter and oil and warm until hot. Working in batches to avoid crowding, add the chicken pieces and cook, turning as needed, until browned, about 10 minutes. Transfer to a plate and set aside.

QUICK COOK If you have included the browning step, pour off all but 2 tablespoons of the fat from the insert and return the insert to medium-high heat. If you are starting here, put the slow-cooker insert on the stove top over medium-high heat, then add the oil and warm until hot. Add the onions and bell pepper and cook, stirring, until softened, about 5 minutes. Stir in the broth, paprika(s), and tomatoes and deglaze the insert, stirring and scraping up the browned bits on the insert bottom with a wooden spoon.

SLOW COOK Transfer the insert to the slow cooker, add the chicken, and stir and turn the chicken pieces to coat with the tomato mixture. Cover and cook on the low-heat setting for 6 hours. The chicken should be tender and opaque throughout.

ASSEMBLE Transfer the chicken to a platter and tent with aluminum foil to keep warm. Bring the liquid to a simmer on the high-heat setting and cook, uncovered, until slightly thickened, about 10 minutes. Turn off the cooker, stir in the sour cream, and season with salt and pepper.

SERVE Transfer the chicken to individual plates, top with the sauce, and serve right away.

Braised Chicken
with
Saffron Rice

This comforting one-dish meal uses a whole chicken, so everyone can choose their favorite part. Nestled in the slow cooker along with rice, savory vegetables, and herbs, it's a crowd-pleasing dish. If you like, add 2 chopped roasted red bell peppers to the rice during the last 15 minutes of cooking. Serve roasted asparagus on the side.

ingredients

Large pinch of saffron threads

½ cup (4 fl oz/125 ml) plus 3 tablespoons dry white wine

1 chicken, about 4–5 lb (2–2.5 kg), cut into 8 serving pieces, trimmed of excess skin and fat

Kosher salt and freshly ground pepper

2 tablespoons olive oil

1 large yellow onion, finely chopped

3 bay leaves

5 cloves garlic, finely chopped

1 teaspoon dried oregano

4 cups (32 fl oz/1 l) low-sodium chicken broth

2 cups (14 oz/440 g) long-grain white rice

2 large jarred roasted red peppers, seeded and chopped (about 1½ cups/9 oz/280 g)

makes 6–8 servings

step by step

PREP In a small bowl, soak the saffron in the 3 tablespoons wine. Season the chicken generously with salt and pepper.

BUILD FLAVOR (OPTIONAL) Put the slow-cooker insert on the stove top over medium-high heat, then add the oil and warm until hot. Working in batches to avoid crowding, add the chicken and cook, turning as needed, until browned, about 10 minutes. Transfer to a plate and set aside.

QUICK COOK If you have included the browning step, pour off all but 2 tablespoons of the fat from the insert and return the insert to medium-high heat. If you are starting here, put the slow-cooker insert on the stove top over medium-high heat, then add the oil and warm until hot. Add the onion and bay leaves and cook, stirring, until the onion is golden, about 6 minutes. Add the garlic and cook, stirring, for 1 minute. Add the oregano, ½ teaspoon salt, several grinds of pepper, the saffron mixture, and the remaining ½ cup wine and deglaze the insert, stirring and scraping up the browned bits on the insert bottom with a wooden spoon.

SLOW COOK Transfer the insert to the slow cooker, add the chicken, broth, and rice, and stir to coat with the saffron-wine mixture. Cover and cook on the low-heat setting for 3 hours. The chicken should be tender and opaque throughout and the rice should be tender.

Uncover and check to be sure a little liquid is still visible at the bottom of the cooker. If it appears dry, add 1 tablespoon water. Sprinkle the roasted pepper evenly over the rice, then re-cover and cook on the low-heat setting for 15 minutes.

SERVE Spoon the chicken and rice onto a platter or individual plates. Serve right away.

Cuban Citrus Chicken

This dish, inspired by the flavors of Cuba, features bold flavors and makes good use of fresh citrus juice. Here, orange and lime juice combined with garlic, onion, and bay form a simple but bold base for an easy main course. Serve with black beans, mashed sweet potatoes, and sliced avocados drizzled with lime juice.

ingredients

1 chicken, 4–5 lb (2–2.5 kg), cut into 8 serving pieces, trimmed of excess skin and fat

Kosher salt and freshly ground pepper

2 tablespoons olive oil

8 cloves garlic, coarsely chopped

¾ cup (6 fl oz/180 ml) fresh orange juice

¾ cup (6 fl oz/ 180 ml), lime juice, from about 5 limes, plus 2 limes, cut into wedges, for serving

1 bay leaf

1 yellow onion, thinly sliced

Chopped fresh cilantro, for garnish

makes 6 servings

step by step

PREP Season the chicken generously with salt and pepper.

BUILD FLAVOR (OPTIONAL) Put the slow-cooker insert on the stove top over medium-high heat, then add the oil and warm until hot. Working in batches to avoid crowding, add the chicken, skin side down, and cook until golden brown on the bottom, about 7 minutes. Turn the chicken and cook on the second side until lightly browned, about 3 minutes longer. Transfer to a plate and set aside.

QUICK COOK If you have included the browning step, pour off all but 2 tablespoons of the fat in the insert. If you are starting here, put the slow-cooker insert on the stove top over medium-high heat, then add the oil and warm until hot. Add the garlic and cook, stirring, just until fragrant, about 1 minute. Pour in the orange and lime juices and raise the heat to high. Bring to a boil and deglaze the insert, stirring and scraping up the browned bits on the insert bottom with a wooden spoon.

SLOW COOK Transfer the insert to the slow cooker and add the chicken and the bay leaf. Spread the onion evenly over the chicken and sprinkle with 1 teaspoon salt. Cover and cook on the low-heat setting for 6 hours. The chicken should be tender and opaque throughout. Remove and discard the bay leaf.

SERVE Transfer the chicken to a platter and spoon the sauce over the top. Serve right away. Pass the cilantro and lime wedges at the table.

Garlic Chicken

Four heads of garlic might sound excessive, but as the cloves cook, they
mellow and thicken the pan juices in this simple braise, adding a sweet flavor.
You do not need to go through the trouble of peeling the garlic cloves, as the
cooking liquid is strained before serving. Serve roasted root vegetables alongside.

ingredients

1 chicken, 4–5 lb (2–2.5 kg), cut into
8 serving pieces, trimmed of excess
skin and fat

Kosher salt and freshly ground pepper

2 tablespoons canola oil

4 heads garlic, separated into cloves,
unpeeled

¼ cup (2 fl oz/60 ml) dry white wine

1 tablespoon chopped fresh thyme

makes 4–6 servings

step by step

PREP Season the chicken with salt and pepper.

BUILD FLAVOR (OPTIONAL) Put the slow-cooker insert on the stove top
over medium-high heat, then add the oil and warm until hot. Working in
batches to avoid crowding, add the chicken and cook, turning as needed,
until browned, about 10 minutes. Transfer to a plate and set aside.

QUICK COOK If you have included the browning step, pour off all but
2 tablespoons of the fat from the insert and return the insert to medium-
high heat. If you are starting here, put the slow-cooker insert on the stove
top over medium-high heat, then add the oil and warm until hot. Add the
garlic and cook, stirring, until lightly browned, about 3 minutes. Pour in
the wine and deglaze the insert, stirring and scraping up the browned
bits on the insert bottom with a wooden spoon.

SLOW COOK Transfer the insert to the slow cooker, add the chicken,
and stir to combine with the garlic-wine sauce. Sprinkle with the thyme.
Cover and cook on the low-heat setting for 6 hours. The chicken should
be tender and opaque throughout.

ASSEMBLE Transfer the chicken to a platter and tent with aluminum
foil to keep warm. Strain the cooking liquid through a fine-mesh sieve
into a small saucepan, pressing on the garlic cloves to extract as much
liquid and pulp as possible. Bring to a simmer over medium-high heat
and season with salt and pepper.

SERVE Spoon the hot liquid over the chicken and serve right away.

Seafood

Smoky Fish Chowder

with

Potatoes and Corn

Thick, rich, and creamy, this is everything you want your fish chowder to be.
Tender bites of potato, sweet kernels of corn, and bits of red bell pepper
provide a hearty base for a mixture of smoked salmon and flaky white cod.
Serve the chowder with corn muffins or thick slices of crusty sourdough bread.

ingredients

2 slices thick-cut applewood-smoked bacon, chopped

1 yellow onion, finely chopped

2 ribs celery, finely chopped

1 red bell pepper, seeded and finely chopped

2 lb (1 kg) Yukon gold potatoes, unpeeled, cut into 1-inch (2.5-cm) pieces

4 cups (32 fl oz/1 l) low-sodium vegetable or chicken broth

½ cup (4 fl oz/125 ml) dry white wine

Kosher salt

2 lb (1 kg) thick white fish fillets such as cod or halibut, cut into 1¼-inch (3-cm) chunks

½ lb (250 g) hot-smoked salmon, skinned and broken into bite-size chunks

1½ cups (9 oz/280 g) frozen white corn

¾ cup (6 fl oz/180 ml) heavy cream

1 bunch fresh chives, chopped (optional)

makes 8 servings

step by step

QUICK COOK Put the slow-cooker insert on the stove top over medium heat, then add the bacon and fry until the bacon is crisp, about 5 minutes. Using a slotted spoon, transfer to a small bowl. Pour off all but 1 tablespoon of the fat from the insert and return the insert to medium-high heat. Add the onion, celery, and bell pepper and cook, stirring often and scraping up any browned bits from the insert bottom with a wooden spoon, until softened, about 3 minutes. Return the bacon to the insert.

SLOW COOK Transfer the insert to the slow cooker, add the potatoes, broth, wine, and 1 teaspoon salt, and stir to mix well. Cover and cook on the low-heat setting for 4 hours. The potatoes should be tender.

Uncover, add the white fish, salmon, corn, and cream, and stir to mix well. Re-cover and cook on the low-heat setting for 1 hour. The white fish should be opaque throughout. Taste and adjust the seasoning with salt.

SERVE Ladle into individual bowls and garnish with the chives, if using. Serve right away.

Indian Fish Curry

This enchanting curry boasts a vivid yellow color and bright flavors from a medley of spices. The fish itself cooks in very little time, but slowly simmering the sauce in advance helps the flavors of the spices to bloom. Serve over hot cooked basmati rice.

ingredients

⅓ cup (3 fl oz/80 ml) canola oil

1 yellow onion, finely chopped

2 cloves garlic, minced

2 small hot green chiles, seeded and minced

1-inch (2.5-cm) piece fresh ginger, peeled and grated

1 tablespoon ground cumin

2 teaspoons ground coriander

2 teaspoons brown mustard seeds

2 teaspoons ground turmeric

2 tomatoes, seeded and chopped

1 tablespoon sugar

Kosher salt

2 lb (1 kg) firm, mild white fish fillets such as tilapia, cod, or halibut, cut into 1-inch (2.5-cm) chunks

3 tablespoons chopped fresh cilantro

makes 6—8 servings

step by step

QUICK COOK Place the slow-cooker insert on the stove top over medium-high heat, then add the oil and warm until hot. Add the onion and cook, stirring, until it begins to turn golden, 5—7 minutes. Stir in the garlic, chiles, ginger, cumin, coriander, mustard, and turmeric and cook, stirring, until the spices are fragrant and evenly coat the onion, about 1 minute. Add the tomatoes, sugar, and 1 teaspoon salt and cook, stirring, until the tomatoes begin to release their juices, about 1 minute. Pour in 1½ cups (12 fl oz/375 ml) water and deglaze the insert, stirring and scraping up the browned bits on the insert bottom with a wooden spoon. Bring to a boil.

SLOW COOK Transfer the insert to the slow cooker. Cover and cook on the low-heat setting for 2 hours. Check the sauce halfway through the total cooking time; if it seems to be getting too thick, stir in more water, about ½ cup (4 fl oz/125 ml) at a time. Uncover and add the fish, stirring gently to coat it with the sauce. Re-cover and continue to cook on the low-heat setting for about 30 minutes longer. The fish should be opaque throughout and the sauce should be thick. Season with salt.

SERVE Transfer the curry to individual bowls and garnish with the cilantro. Serve right away.

Halibut
with
Peperonata

Light and colorful, this festive dish is the perfect main course for a hot summer evening. Accompany the fish with thick slices of grilled coarse country bread and wilted greens tossed with sautéed garlic and red pepper flakes.

ingredients

2 tablespoons olive oil

1 large red onion, finely chopped

2 red bell peppers, seeded and cut into ¼-inch (6-mm) dice

2 yellow or orange bell peppers, seeded and cut into ¼-inch (6-mm) dice

1 tablespoon minced garlic

2 tablespoons tomato paste

½ cup (4 fl oz/125 ml) fruity white wine such as Pinot Grigio

1 cup (8 fl oz/250 ml) bottled clam juice

1 can (14 oz/440 g) whole plum tomatoes with juice

¼ cup (2 fl oz/60 ml) balsamic vinegar

1 teaspoon fennel seeds

Kosher and freshly ground pepper

2 lb (1 kg) halibut or other firm white fish fillets, cut into 4 equal portions

⅓ cup (½ oz/15 g) finely chopped fresh parsley leaves

3 tablespoons unsalted butter

makes 4 servings

step by step

QUICK COOK Put the slow-cooker insert on the stove top over medium-high heat, then add the oil and warm until hot. Add the onion, red and yellow peppers, and garlic and cook, stirring, until softened, about 5 minutes. Whisk in the tomato paste and cook, stirring, for 1 minute. Pour in the wine and simmer until evaporated, 2–3 minutes. Add the clam juice, tomatoes, vinegar, fennel seeds, 1 teaspoon salt, and a few grinds of pepper and bring to a boil. Crush the tomatoes with a potato masher and boil for 2 minutes.

SLOW COOK Transfer the insert to the slow cooker, cover, and cook on the high-heat setting for 2 hours. The bell peppers should be very tender.

Season the fish lightly with salt and pepper. Uncover the cooker and add the fish. Re-cover and continue to cook on the high-heat setting for 1 hour. The fish should be opaque throughout yet still firm.

ASSEMBLE Transfer the fish to a plate and cover loosely to keep warm. Add the parsley and butter to the sauce and stir until the butter melts, then taste and adjust the seasoning with salt and pepper if needed.

SERVE Transfer the fish to individual plates and spoon the sauce over the top. Serve right away.

Herbed Salmon
and
Green Beans

Highly nutritious salmon becomes melt-in-your-mouth tender after a short braise in the slow cooker. While the salmon is cooking, slender green beans are cooked just until tender, then tossed with finely chopped shallot and fresh tarragon, providing a brightly flavored counterpoint to the meaty fish.

ingredients

½ cup (4 fl oz/125 ml) low-sodium vegetable broth

1 cup (8 fl oz/250 ml) dry white wine

½ small yellow onion, sliced

3 sprigs fresh tarragon, plus 1 teaspoon minced tarragon

Kosher salt and freshly ground pepper

6 salmon fillets, each about 5 oz (155 g)

1 lb (500 g) slender green beans, trimmed

1 tablespoon unsalted butter

1 tablespoon olive oil

1 large shallot, minced

2 teaspoons white wine vinegar

makes 6 servings

step by step

SLOW COOK In the slow cooker, stir together ½ cup (4 fl oz/125 ml) water with the broth, wine, onion, tarragon sprigs, ½ teaspoon salt, and several grinds of pepper. Cover and cook on the low-heat setting for 30 minutes to blend the flavors.

Uncover and add the salmon fillets (they can overlap). Re-cover and continue to cook on the low-heat setting for 45—60 minutes. The fish should be opaque throughout yet still firm.

ASSEMBLE About 15 minutes before the salmon is ready, bring a large saucepan three-fourths full of lightly salted water to a boil. Add the green beans and cook until tender-crisp, 4—5 minutes. Drain and hold under cold running water until cool, then spread on a kitchen towel to dry. In a frying pan over medium heat, melt the butter with the oil. Add the shallot and cook, stirring, until slightly softened, 2—3 minutes. Add the beans and stir until hot throughout. Add the vinegar and minced tarragon and toss to mix well.

SERVE Transfer the salmon to individual plates. Discard the braising liquid. Arrange a mound of the green beans alongside each salmon fillet. Serve right away.

Braised Salmon
with
Tamari, Lemon, and Ginger

This is so fast and easy—and delicious—that it's certain to become one of your regular menu items. The mix of tart lemon, spicy ginger, salty tamari, and sweet brown sugar infuses the salmon with big flavors. Serve with a quick sauté of sugar snap peas and some steamed rice for soaking up the juices.

ingredients

¼ cup (2 fl oz/60 ml) tamari or low-sodium soy sauce

Finely grated zest of 1 large lemon

Juice of 2 large lemons

1 heaping tablespoon peeled and grated fresh ginger

2 tablespoons firmly packed golden brown sugar

6 salmon fillets with skin intact, about 6 oz (185 g) each

makes 6 servings

step by step

PREP In the slow-cooker insert, combine the tamari, lemon zest and juice, ginger, and brown sugar and stir until the sugar dissolves. Add the salmon fillets and turn to coat evenly with the sauce, then turn skin side down. Let stand at room temperature for 15 minutes.

SLOW COOK Transfer the insert to the slow cooker, cover, and cook on the low-heat setting for 45—60 minutes. The fish should be opaque throughout yet still firm.

SERVE Transfer the salmon to a platter. Strain the cooking liquid through a fine-mesh sieve into a small bowl and set alongside the platter. Serve right away.

Salmon Fillets
with
Cucumber-Yogurt Sauce

The slow cooker brings out the succulent texture of salmon, a fish rich in good-for-you oils. These natural oils mean that a long, gentle cooking time makes the salmon surprisingly light and meltingly tender. An easy cucumber-yogurt mixture doubles as both a sauce and a salad, rounding out the meal.

ingredients

½ cup (4 fl oz/125 ml) low-sodium vegetable broth

1 cup (8 fl oz/250 ml) dry white wine

½ small yellow onion, sliced

3 sprigs fresh dill, plus 4 tablespoons (⅓ oz/10 g) coarsely chopped dill

Kosher salt and freshly ground pepper

6 salmon fillets, each about 5 oz (155 g)

1 cup (8 oz/250 g) plain yogurt

1 tablespoon mayonnaise

1 shallot, minced

4 tablespoons (⅓ oz/10 g) coarsely chopped fresh flat-leaf parsley

¼ teaspoon ground cumin

1 English cucumber, halved lengthwise and thinly sliced crosswise

makes 6 servings

step by step

SLOW COOK In a slow cooker, stir together ½ cup (4 fl oz/125 ml) water with the broth, wine, onion, dill sprigs, ½ teaspoon salt, and several grinds of pepper. Cover and cook on the low-heat setting for 30 minutes to blend the flavors.

Uncover and add the salmon fillets (they can overlap). Re-cover and continue to cook on the low-heat setting for 45—60 minutes. The fish should be opaque throughout yet still firm.

ASSEMBLE About 10 minutes before the salmon is ready, in a bowl, whisk together the yogurt, mayonnaise, shallot, 3 tablespoons of the chopped dill, 3 tablespoons of the parsley, and the cumin. Add the cucumber and mix well. Season with salt and pepper.

SERVE Transfer the salmon fillets to individual plates. Discard the braising liquid. Spoon the cucumber-yogurt salad over the salmon, dividing it evenly. Garnish with the remaining dill and parsley and serve right away.

Coconut Fish Curry

The mix of spices, the tang of tamarind chutney, and the creaminess of the coconut milk elevate this Indian-inspired curry to dinner-party status. Serve it over steamed basmati rice or with toasted whole-wheat Indian bread. If you can find fresh curry leaves, add 4—5 leaves with the other spices, then remove them just before serving.

ingredients

1 tablespoon canola oil

1 small or ½ large yellow onion, finely chopped

Kosher salt

2 tomatoes, seeded and finely chopped

3 tablespoons tamarind chutney

1 heaping tablespoon peeled and grated fresh ginger

1 teaspoon ground coriander

1 teaspoon ancho or other medium-hot chile powder

1 teaspoon yellow mustard seeds

½ teaspoon ground turmeric

1 can (13½ fl oz/420 ml) coconut milk, shaken well before opening

2 lb (1 kg) thick halibut or cod fillets, cut into 1½-inch (4-cm) pieces

makes 6 servings

step by step

QUICK COOK Put the slow-cooker insert on the stove top over medium heat, then add the oil and warm until hot. Add the onion and a pinch of salt and cook, stirring, until lightly golden, about 5 minutes. Add the tomatoes, chutney, ginger, coriander, chile powder, mustard, turmeric, and 1 teaspoon salt and cook, stirring, until the tomatoes start to break down and the spices are fragrant, about 5 minutes.

SLOW COOK Transfer the insert to the slow cooker, add the coconut milk, and stir to mix well. Add the fish and again stir to mix well. Cover and cook on the low-heat setting for 1 hour. The fish should be opaque throughout yet still firm.

SERVE Spoon onto plates and serve right away.

Sri Lankan Fish Stew

Coconut milk adds a touch of the tropics to this mildly spiced dish, and tamarind paste contributes a sour-sweet flavor. You can make the stew with any mild, firm fish fillets, but rosy-hued salmon looks especially pretty in contrast to the creamy golden sauce. Accompany the stew with steamed white rice.

ingredients

2 tablespoons canola oil

1 yellow onion, chopped

3 cloves garlic, minced

½ teaspoon cayenne pepper

½ teaspoon ground coriander

½ teaspoon ground turmeric

¼ teaspoon ground cumin

¼ teaspoon freshly ground black pepper

¼ teaspoon fennel seeds

Pinch of ground cinnamon

Pinch of ground cloves

2 tomatoes, seeded and chopped

1 can (13½ oz/420 ml) coconut milk, shaken well before opening

1 tablespoon tamarind paste dissolved in 3 tablespoons warm water

1 teaspoon sugar

Kosher salt

2 lb (1 kg) salmon, halibut, or sea bass fillets, cut into serving pieces

makes 6—8 servings

step by step

QUICK COOK Place the slow-cooker insert on the stove top over medium-high heat, then add the oil and warm until hot. Add the onion and garlic and cook, stirring, until they begin to soften, about 3 minutes. Add the cayenne, coriander, turmeric, cumin, black pepper, fennel, cinnamon, and cloves and cook, stirring, until the spices are fragrant and evenly coat the onion and garlic, about 30 seconds. Add the tomatoes and sauté until they start to release their juices, about 1 minute. Stir in the coconut milk, dissolved tamarind paste, sugar, and ¾ teaspoon salt. Bring to a boil, and deglaze the insert, stirring and scraping up the browned bits on the insert bottom with a wooden spoon.

SLOW COOK Transfer the insert to the slow cooker. Cover and cook on the low-heat setting for 3 hours. The sauce should be thick but still fluid. Uncover and add the fish, stirring gently to coat it with the sauce. Re-cover and continue to cook on the low-heat setting for about 30 minutes longer. The fish should flake but still be very moist and the sauce should be thick.

SERVE Transfer the fish to individual plates and spoon the sauce over the top. Serve right away.

Fish and Shrimp Stew
with
Fennel, Leeks, and Saffron

Saffron adds a floral note and lovely yellow hue to this hearty stew that recalls the cuisine of southern France. To complete the menu, set out a crusty loaf of French bread, a simple green salad, and a bottle of the same wine you used in the stew.

ingredients

2 tablespoons unsalted butter

1 small red onion, finely chopped

½ fennel bulb, minced

1 leek, white and pale green part, very thinly sliced

2 teaspoons minced garlic

3 tablespoons all-purpose flour

3 tablespoons tomato paste

½ cup (4 fl oz/125 ml) fruity white wine such as Sauvignon Blanc

1½ cups (12 fl oz/375 ml) bottled clam juice

1 can (14 oz/440 g) whole plum tomatoes with juice

¼ cup (2 fl oz/60 ml) fresh orange juice

½ teaspoon crushed saffron threads

Kosher salt and freshly ground pepper

1 lb (500 g) large shrimp, peeled and deveined

1 lb (500 g) firm white fish fillets such as cod, cut into 1-inch pieces

¼ cup (⅓ oz/10 g) finely chopped fresh flat-leaf parsley

makes 4 servings

step by step

QUICK COOK Put the slow-cooker insert on the stove top over medium heat, then add the butter and warm until melted. Add the onion, fennel, leek, and garlic and cook, stirring, until softened, about 5 minutes. Whisk in the flour and tomato paste and cook, stirring, until the flour is fully incorporated, about 30 seconds. Add the wine and simmer until evaporated, 2–3 minutes. Add the clam juice, tomatoes, orange juice, saffron, 1 teaspoon salt, and a few grinds of pepper and bring to a boil. Crush the tomatoes with a potato masher, then boil for 2 minutes.

SLOW COOK Transfer the insert to the slow cooker, cover, and cook on the low-heat setting for 4 hours. The fennel and leek should be tender and the mixture should be aromatic.

Uncover, add the shrimp, fish, and parsley, and stir to mix well. Re-cover the cooker and cook on the low-heat setting for 1 hour. The shrimp and fish should be opaque.

SERVE Spoon into shallow individual bowls and serve right away.

Clay Pot Fish

Two seemingly contradictory flavors—intensely sweet caramel and briny fish sauce—harmonize beautifully in the sauce of this Vietnamese-inspired dish. Fish fillets, added during the last half hour of cooking, not only soak up the flavors but also acquire a deep, glossy mahogany color. Accompany with steamed jasmine rice.

ingredients

½ cup (4 oz/125 g) sugar

¼ cup (2 fl oz/60 ml) canola oil

3 cloves garlic, minced

3 shallots, minced

1-inch (2.5-cm) piece fresh ginger, peeled and grated

2 fresh small hot red chiles, halved lengthwise, seeded, and thinly sliced crosswise

¼ cup (2 fl oz/60 ml) Asian fish sauce

¼ cup (2 fl oz/60 ml) low-sodium soy sauce

2 lb (1 kg) firm, mild white fish fillets such as black cod or halibut, cut into 1-inch (2.5-cm) chunks

Freshly ground pepper

makes 6–8 servings

step by step

PREP Put the slow-cooker insert on the stove top over medium-high heat, then add the sugar and ¼ cup (2 fl oz/60 ml) water. Cook, stirring occasionally, until the sugar melts, then bring to a boil, stirring frequently. Continue to boil, stirring frequently, until the mixture turns caramel brown, 12–15 minutes. Watch carefully to prevent burning. Remove from the heat and, taking care to avoid splatters, stir in ¼ cup water until thoroughly blended. Pour into a small heatproof bowl and set aside. Rinse the insert.

QUICK COOK Put the insert on the stove top over medium-high heat, then add the oil and warm until hot. Add the garlic, shallots, ginger, and chiles and cook, stirring, just until tender, 1–2 minutes. Stir in the fish sauce, soy sauce, reserved caramel, and 1 cup (8 fl oz/250 ml) water and bring to a boil, stirring occasionally.

SLOW COOK Transfer the insert to the slow cooker. Cover and cook on the low-heat setting for 1–1½ hours. The sauce should be syrupy but still fluid. If the sauce becomes too thick, stir in ½ cup (4 fl oz/125 ml) water.

Uncover, add the fish, and stir gently to coat with the sauce. Re-cover and cook, turning the fish once at the midway point, for about 25 minutes longer. The fish should be opaque throughout. Season with pepper.

SERVE Transfer the fish and sauce to individual plates and serve right away.

Seafood Gumbo

This shrimp and crab stew is representative of just one of the many types of gumbo you'll find in the New Orleans area. For an authentic touch, pass filé powder at the table and instruct guests to stir it into their stew a little at a time to thicken it to their taste. You can also add green Tabasco sauce for a little extra heat.

ingredients

¼ cup (2 fl oz/60 ml) canola oil

¼ cup (1 oz/30 g) all-purpose flour

1 yellow onion, finely chopped

1 green bell pepper, seeded and finely chopped

2 ribs celery, finely chopped

1 tablespoon minced garlic

½ jalapeño chile, minced

¼ cup (2 oz/60 g) tomato paste

1 bottle (12 fl oz/375 ml) pale lager

2 cups (16 fl oz/500 ml) bottled clam juice

⅛ teaspoon cayenne pepper

Kosher salt and freshly ground black pepper

1 lb (500 g) large shrimp, peeled and deveined

1 lb (500 g) lump crabmeat, picked over for shell fragments

½ cup (¾ oz/20 g) finely chopped fresh flat-leaf parsley

1½ cups long-grain white rice

Filé powder

makes 4 servings

step by step

QUICK COOK Put the slow-cooker insert on the stove top over medium-high heat, then add the oil and warm until hot. Gradually whisk in the flour and cook, whisking constantly, until the mixture is light tan, about 5 minutes. Add the onion, bell pepper, celery, garlic, and chile and cook, stirring, until soft, about 5 minutes. Add the tomato paste and whisk until fully incorporated, about 30 seconds. Pour in the lager and simmer for 3 minutes. Add the clam juice, cayenne, 1 teaspoon salt, and a few grinds of black pepper and bring to a boil.

SLOW COOK Transfer the insert to the slow cooker. Cover and cook on the low-heat setting for 4 hours. The mixture should be aromatic and the bell pepper should be soft.

Uncover, add the shrimp, crabmeat, and parsley, and stir gently to mix well. Re-cover and continue to cook on the low-heat setting for 30—60 minutes, or until the shrimp is opaque.

ASSEMBLE About 20 minutes before the gumbo is ready, steam the rice according to your favorite method, on the stove top or in a rice cooker.

SERVE Spoon the gumbo into individual bowls and serve right away. Pass the rice and filé powder at the table.

Smoky Jambalaya
with
Shrimp, Chicken, and Ham

This is a great dish to make when you will be away with the family for the afternoon. When all of you return home, the whole house will be filled with the aromas of this iconic Creole dish and dinner will be ready. Serve with a big green salad.

ingredients

2 tablespoons olive oil

12 large shrimp, about 10 oz (315 g) total weight, peeled and deveined

2 skinless, boneless chicken breast halves, 4–6 oz (125–185 g) each, cut into large pieces

1 yellow onion, finely chopped

1 green bell pepper, seeded and chopped

2 ribs celery, finely chopped

1 clove garlic, minced

1 jalapeño chile, minced

2 tomatoes, seeded and chopped

1 cup (7 oz/220 g) long-grain white rice

2 cups (16 fl oz/500 ml) low-sodium chicken broth

Kosher salt and freshly ground black pepper

6 oz (185 g) smoked ham, cut into ½-inch (12-mm) cubes

1 teaspoon sweet paprika

1 tablespoon chopped fresh thyme

Pinch of cayenne pepper, or more to taste

makes 4–6 servings

step by step

BUILD FLAVOR (OPTIONAL) Put the slow-cooker insert on the stove top over medium-high heat, then add the oil and warm until hot. Add the shrimp and cook, turning once, until opaque, about 3 minutes on each side. Transfer to a plate and set aside to cool for about 5 minutes. Add the chicken pieces to the fat remaining in the insert and cook, turning as needed, until browned, about 5 minutes. Transfer to another plate. Cover and refrigerate the shrimp until needed. Pour off the fat from the insert.

QUICK COOK If you have included the browning step, pour off all but 2 tablespoons fat from the insert and return it to medium-high heat. If you are starting from here, put the slow cooker insert on the stove top over medium-high heat, then add the 2 tablespoons oil and warm until hot. Add the onion, bell pepper, and celery and cook, stirring, until softened, about 5 minutes. Do not allow to brown. Add the garlic and chile and cook, stirring, until fragrant, about 1 minute.

SLOW COOK Transfer the insert to the slow cooker and stir in the chicken, tomatoes, rice, broth, and a pinch of salt. Cover and cook on the low-heat setting for 3 hours. The chicken should be opaque throughout, the rice should be tender, and the broth should be absorbed.

ASSEMBLE Add the shrimp, ham, paprika, thyme, and cayenne to the rice and stir to mix well. Re-cover and cook on the low-heat setting for 30 minutes to warm through. Season with salt and black pepper.

SERVE Spoon into individual bowls and serve right away.

Braised Squid
with
Tomatoes and Fennel

Although this delicious braise is a satisfying main dish, it can also be served in smaller portions as a first course for a Mediterranean-inspired supper. Accompany it with grilled bread rubbed with a cut garlic clove for dipping into the fragrant sauce.

ingredients

2 tablespoons olive oil

1 yellow onion, finely chopped

½ bulb fennel, minced

1 tablespoon minced garlic

3 tablespoons all-purpose flour

3 tablespoons tomato paste

½ cup (4 fl oz/125 ml) fruity white wine such as Pinot Grigio

1½ cups (12 fl oz/375 ml) bottled clam juice

1 can (14 oz/440 g) whole plum tomatoes with juice

Kosher salt and freshly ground pepper

2 lb (1 kg) cleaned squid, bodies and tentacles cut into 1-inch (2.5-cm) pieces

¼ cup (⅓ oz/10 g) finely chopped fresh flat-leaf parsley

makes 4 servings

step by step

QUICK COOK Put the slow-cooker insert on the stove top over medium-high heat, then add the oil and warm until hot. Add the onion, fennel, and garlic and cook, stirring, until softened, about 5 minutes. Whisk in the flour and tomato paste and cook, stirring, until the flour is fully incorporated, about 30 seconds. Add the wine and simmer, stirring occasionally, until evaporated, 2—3 minutes. Add the clam juice, tomatoes and their juice, 1 teaspoon salt, and a few grinds of pepper and bring to a boil. Crush the tomatoes with a potato masher, then boil for 2 minutes.

SLOW COOK Transfer the insert to the slow cooker, cover, and cook on the low-heat setting for 3 hours. The fennel should be tender and the mixture should be aromatic.

Uncover, add the squid and parsley, and stir to mix well. Re-cover and continue to cook on the low-heat setting for 1 hour. The squid should be very tender.

SERVE Spoon into shallow individual bowls and serve right away.

Legumes AND Grains

Vegetarian Chili

Packed with vegetables and legumes, this dish is hearty comfort food at its best, plus
it will satisfy both vegans and meat eaters alike. Serve it with thick slices of warm
corn bread or over freshly steamed rice or a baked potato. You can dress it up with
shredded cheese, a dollop of plain yogurt, and a sprinkling of chopped green onions.

ingredients

2 cans (15 oz/470 g each) pinto beans,
drained and rinsed

2 cans (15 oz/470 g) red kidney beans or
red beans, drained and rinsed

1 can (15 oz/470 g) chickpeas, drained
and rinsed

1 can (28 oz/875 g) crushed tomatoes
with juice

1 can (15 oz/470 g) fire-roasted diced
tomatoes with juice

1 large yellow onion, finely chopped

1 large carrot, peeled and finely chopped

1 small red bell pepper, seeded and
finely chopped

1 small green bell pepper, seeded and
finely chopped

3 tablespoons chili powder

1 tablespoon ground cumin

Kosher salt

2 cups (12 oz/375 g) frozen corn kernels

makes 8 servings

step by step

SLOW COOK In the slower cooker, combine the pinto and kidney beans,
chickpeas, crushed tomatoes, diced tomatoes, onion, carrot, red and green
peppers, chili powder, cumin, 1 tablespoon salt, and 1 cup (8 fl oz/250 ml)
water. Stir to mix well. Cover and cook on the low-heat setting for 6 hours
to blend the flavors.

Uncover, add the corn, and stir well. Re-cover and continue to cook on the
low-heat setting for 30 minutes. The corn should be tender and warmed
through. Taste and adjust the seasoning with salt.

SERVE Transfer to individual bowls and serve right away.

Curried Red Lentil *and* Vegetable Dal

Redolent with the flavors of garlic, ginger, and garam masala, this hearty vegetarian stew—chock full of cauliflower, potatoes, and lentils—will transport you to southern India. Garnish with fresh cilantro and serve with warm naan or other Indian bread.

ingredients

2 tablespoons coconut oil

1 red onion, finely chopped

1 large carrot, peeled and finely chopped

1 tablespoon minced garlic

1 tablespoon peeled and minced fresh ginger

½ jalapeño chile, finely chopped

¼ cup (2 oz/60 g) tomato paste

3 cups (24 fl oz/750 ml) low-sodium vegetable broth

2 cups (16 fl oz/500 ml) strained tomatoes

⅓ cup (4 oz/125 g) mango chutney

2 teaspoons garam masala

Kosher salt and freshly ground pepper

1 rounded cup (8 oz/250 g) red lentils, picked over and rinsed

1½ lb (750 g) small red potatoes, quartered

3 cups (10 oz/315 g) cauliflower florets (about ½ head)

½ cup (⅔ oz/20 g) finely chopped fresh cilantro

makes 6 servings

step by step

QUICK COOK Put the slow-cooker insert on the stove top over medium heat, then add the oil and warm until hot. Add the onion, carrot, garlic, ginger, and chile and cook, stirring, until almost softened, 5–8 minutes. Whisk in the tomato paste and cook, stirring, for 1 minute. Add the broth, tomatoes, chutney, garam masala, 1½ teaspoons salt, and a few grinds of pepper and stir well. Bring to a boil.

SLOW COOK Transfer the insert to the slow cooker, add the lentils and potatoes, and stir to mix well. Cover and cook on the low-heat setting for 5½ hours. The lentils and potatoes should be tender but not falling apart.

Uncover and stir in the cauliflower. Re-cover and cook on the high-heat setting for 1 hour. The cauliflower should be tender.

SERVE Transfer the dal to a serving bowl, garnish with the cilantro, and serve right away.

White Beans
with
Lemon and Rosemary

In Tuscany, slowly simmered, simply seasoned beans are sometimes served as a lunchtime vegetarian main course. For a heartier dish, top these savory beans with excellent quality canned tuna or poached eggs. Round out the menu with a bitter greens salad dressed with a tart vinaigrette.

ingredients

1 lb (500 g) dried cannellini or Great Northern beans

9 cloves garlic, 6 left whole and 3 minced

1 sprig fresh rosemary

½ cup (4 fl oz/125 ml) olive oil

Kosher salt and freshly ground pepper

3 tablespoons finely chopped fresh flat-leaf parsley

2 lemons, each cut into 6 wedges

makes 6–8 servings

step by step

PREP Pick over the beans, removing any misshapen beans or grit. Rinse under cold running water. Put the beans in a large bowl, add cold water to cover by at least 2 inches (5 cm), and let stand at room temperature overnight. Alternatively, for a quick soak, put the beans in a large pot, add water to cover by at least 2 inches, bring to a boil, remove from the heat, cover, and let soak for 1 hour. Drain and rinse the beans. Bring a large kettle filled with water to a boil.

SLOW COOK Transfer the beans to the slow cooker. Bury the whole garlic cloves and the rosemary sprig in the beans. Add boiling water to cover the beans by 1–2 inches (2.5–5 cm). Cover and cook on the low-heat setting for 8 hours. The beans should be very tender.

ASSEMBLE Just before serving, in a small frying pan over medium heat, warm the oil until hot. Add the minced garlic and sauté just until fragrant, about 1 minute. Do not allow to brown. Remove from the heat and keep warm. Drain the beans, discarding the liquid, then remove and discard the rosemary sprig. Season generously with salt and pepper.

SERVE Spoon the beans onto individual plates. Drizzle with the warm garlic oil, garnish with the parsley, and serve right away. Pass the lemon wedges at the table.

Cuban Black Beans and Ham

Black beans, onions, and a trio of colorful bell peppers simmer with a smoky ham hock for a rustic main dish inspired by the cuisine of Cuba. Look for a meaty ham hock, and ask the butcher to cut it in half to release more flavor. For a satisfying supper, top the beans with fried eggs and serve with slices of grilled coarse country bread.

ingredients

1 lb (500 g) dried black beans

1 green bell pepper, seeded and chopped

1 red bell pepper, seeded and chopped

1 yellow bell pepper, seeded and chopped

1 yellow onion, chopped

1 clove garlic, minced

1 smoked ham hock, 6–8 oz (185–250 g)

2 cups (16 fl oz/500 ml) low-sodium chicken broth

2 teaspoons ground cumin

2 teaspoons chopped fresh oregano

Kosher salt and freshly ground pepper

makes 6–8 servings

step by step

PREP Pick over the beans, removing any misshapen beans or grit. Rinse under cold running water. Put the beans in a large bowl, add cold water to cover by at least 2 inches (5 cm), and let stand at room temperature overnight. Alternatively, for a quick soak, put the beans in a large pot, add water to cover by at least 2 inches, bring to a boil, remove from the heat, cover, and let soak for 1 hour. Drain and rinse the beans.

SLOW COOK Transfer the beans to the slow cooker. Add all of the bell peppers, the onion, and garlic and stir well. Add the ham hock, pour in the broth, stir in the cumin and oregano, and season with salt and pepper. Add water to cover the beans by 1 inch (2.5 cm). Cover and cook on the low-heat setting for 6 hours. The beans should be tender but not mushy.

ASSEMBLE Remove the ham hock and re-cover the slow cooker to keep the beans warm. When the ham hock is cool enough to handle, remove as much of the lean meat as possible and discard the skin, fat, and bones. Cut the meat into bite-size pieces as needed, then stir the meat into the hot beans. Season with salt and pepper.

SERVE Transfer to a serving bowl and serve right away.

Indian Chickpea Curry

Pair this boldly flavored chickpea stew with steamed rice for a vegetarian main dish. The addition of garam masala, a widely available blend of spices, at the end of the simmering time heightens the flavor and aroma of the stew. Accompany with a salad of cucumber, tomato, and white onion dressed with lemon juice and cumin.

ingredients

1 lb (500 g) dried chickpeas

2 tablespoons canola oil

1 yellow onion, finely chopped

2 cloves garlic, minced

1-inch (2.5-cm) piece fresh ginger, peeled and grated

2-inch (5-cm) piece cinnamon stick, broken in half

1 teaspoon cayenne pepper

1 teaspoon ground coriander

1 teaspoon ground cumin

1 teaspoon brown mustard seeds

1 teaspoon ground turmeric

1 can (28 oz/875 g) diced tomatoes with juice

2 teaspoons sugar

Kosher salt

1 tablespoon garam masala

1 tablespoon fresh lime juice

1 cup (1⅓ oz/35 g) chopped fresh cilantro

makes 6–8 servings

step by step

PREP Pick over the chickpeas, removing any misshapen chickpeas or grit. Rinse under cold running water. Put the chickpeas in a large bowl, add cold water to cover by at least 2 inches (5 cm), and let stand at room temperature overnight. Alternatively, for a quick soak, put the chickpeas in a large pot, add water to cover by at least 2 inches, bring to a boil, remove from the heat, cover, and let soak for 1 hour. Drain and rinse the chickpeas.

QUICK COOK Put the slow-cooker insert on the stove top over medium-high heat, then add the oil and warm until hot. Add the onion, garlic, and ginger and cook, stirring, until the mixture just begins to turn golden, about 6 minutes. Add the cinnamon, cayenne, coriander, cumin, mustard, and turmeric and cook, stirring, until the spices are fragrant and evenly coat the onion mixture, about 1 minute. Stir in the tomatoes, sugar, and 2 teaspoons salt. Pour in 2 cups (16 fl oz/500 ml) water and deglaze the insert, stirring and scraping up the browned bits on the insert bottom with a wooden spoon. Bring to a boil.

SLOW COOK Transfer the insert to the slow cooker and stir in the chickpeas. Cover and cook on the low-heat setting for 8 hours. The chickpeas should be very tender.

About 15 minutes before the chickpeas are ready, uncover, sprinkle the garam masala and lime juice evenly over the chickpeas, and stir to mix, breaking up some of the chickpeas with the back of the spoon to thicken the mixture slightly. Taste and adjust the seasoning with salt, then re-cover and continue to cook on the low-heat setting for 15 minutes.

SERVE Remove and discard the cinnamon stick. Transfer the chickpeas to a serving bowl, garnish with the cilantro, and serve right away.

Barbecue Beans and Pork

The addition of the pork shoulder makes this dish robust and hearty, but you can make this dish vegan by leaving out both the pork shoulder and the bacon and using vegetable broth in place of the chicken broth. Look for a good-quality barbecue sauce that isn't overly sweet or purchase a jar from a local BBQ joint where you like what is served. Accompany the dish with warm cornbread or garlic toast and creamy coleslaw.

ingredients

1 lb (500 g) dried white beans such as navy or Great Northern

¼ lb (125 g) thick-cut pepper bacon slices, cut into ½-inch (12-mm) pieces

1 lb (500 g) boneless pork shoulder, in a single piece

1 yellow onion, finely chopped

1 small green bell pepper, seeded and finely chopped

2½–3 cups (20–24 fl oz/625–750 ml) good-quality bottled barbecue sauce

1 cup (8 fl oz/250 ml) low-sodium chicken or beef broth

2 tablespoons whole-grain mustard

¼ cup (2 oz/60 g) firmly packed golden brown sugar (optional)

makes 6–8 servings

step by step

PREP Pick over the white beans, removing any misshapen beans or grit. Rinse under cold running water. Put the beans in a large bowl, add cold water to cover by at least 2 inches (5 cm), and let stand at room temperature overnight. Alternatively, for a quick soak, put the beans in a large pot, add water to cover by at least 2 inches, bring to a boil, remove from the heat, cover, and let soak for 1 hour. Drain and rinse the beans.

QUICK COOK Put the slow-cooker insert over medium heat, then add the bacon and fry until the fat is rendered and the bacon is crisp, about 5 minutes. Using a slotted spoon, transfer the bacon to paper towels to drain. Add the pork shoulder to the fat remaining in the insert and cook over medium heat, turning once, until well browned on both sides, about 5 minutes on each side. Transfer the pork to a plate. Pour off the fat from the insert.

SLOW COOK Transfer the insert to the slow cooker, add the drained beans, onion, bell pepper, barbecue sauce, broth, mustard, and the bacon. If the barbecue sauce is very sweet, do not add the sugar; if it is not very sweet, add the sugar, then stir together all of the ingredients to mix well. Nestle the pork in the bean mixture. Cover and cook on the low-heat setting for 8 hours, stirring occasionally if possible. Switch to the high-heat setting and cook for 1–3 hours longer, stirring 2 or 3 times if possible. The beans should be very tender and the sauce should be thickened to your liking. The longer the mixture cooks, the thicker the sauce will become.

ASSEMBLE Transfer the meat to a cutting board. Using 2 forks, shred the meat into bite-size pieces, discarding any large pieces of fat. Return the meat to the slow cooker and stir to combine.

SERVE Spoon the pork and beans into a large serving bowl and serve right away.

Herbed Lentil Soup

One of the best things about lentils is that, unlike many dried legumes, you don't need to soak them overnight. This soup is packed with ingredients that you don't normally see in the same recipe—cumin, tomato paste, fresh dill—but that work together beautifully here. Serve with a soft cheese like Brie and slices of toasted baguette.

ingredients

2 tablespoons olive oil

1 large yellow onion, finely chopped

1 carrot, peeled and finely chopped

2 ribs celery, finely chopped

5 cloves garlic, thinly sliced

1 teaspoon ground cumin

1 teaspoon dried oregano

1 tablespoon tomato paste

½ cup (4 fl oz/125 ml) dry red wine

6 cups (48 fl oz/1.5 l) low-sodium chicken broth

1 lb (500 g) brown lentils, picked over and rinsed

¼ lb (125 g) cooked ham, finely diced

Kosher salt and freshly ground pepper

1 tablespoon chopped fresh dill

makes 6—8 servings

step by step

QUICK COOK Put the slow-cooker insert on the stove top over medium-high heat, then add the oil and warm until hot. Add the onion, carrot, and celery and cook, stirring, until softened and just beginning to brown, about 6 minutes. Stir in the garlic, cumin, and oregano and cook, stirring, for about 1 minute, then stir in the tomato paste and cook, stirring, for 1 minute longer. Pour in the wine and 1 cup (8 fl oz/250 ml) of the broth and deglaze the insert, stirring and scraping up the browned bits on the insert bottom with a wooden spoon.

SLOW COOK Transfer the insert to the slow cooker and stir in the remaining 5 cups (40 fl oz/1.25 l) broth, the lentils, the ham, ¼ teaspoon salt, and several grinds of pepper. Cover and cook on the low-heat setting for 5 hours. The lentils should be very tender.

ASSEMBLE Let the soup cool slightly. Transfer about one-third of the soup to a food processor or blender and process until smooth. Return the purée to the soup and stir well.

SERVE Ladle the soup into shallow individual bowls. Sprinkle each serving with a little pepper and scatter the dill over the top. Serve right away.

Hearty Split Pea Soup

A slow cooker is the perfect way to prepare this classic recipe for split pea soup. After a quick sauté to bring out the flavor of the aromatics, the soup simmers slowly for the length of a workday. Accompany the soup with warm focaccia or toasted country levain bread and a tossed green salad, if you like.

ingredients

1 lb (500 g) green split peas, picked over and rinsed

1 yellow onion, finely chopped

2 ribs celery, finely chopped

6 cups (48 fl oz/1.5 l) low-sodium chicken broth

2 tablespoons dry white wine

1 smoked ham hock, about 1½ lb (750 g)

Kosher salt and freshly ground pepper

makes 6—8 servings

step by step

PREP Pick over the split peas, removing any misshapen peas or grit. Rinse under cold running water.

SLOW COOK Transfer the split peas to the slow cooker, Add the onion, celery, broth, and wine and stir to mix well. Add the ham hock, cover, and cook on the low-heat setting for 9 hours. The split peas should be very tender.

ASSEMBLE Remove the ham hock, let cool until it can be handled, then pull off the meat and discard the skin, bone, and cartilage. Using 2 forks, shred the meat into bite-size pieces and set aside. Transfer about one-third of the soup to a blender or food processor and process until smooth. Return the purée to the slow cooker, add the reserved meat, and stir well. Season with salt and pepper, then cover and rewarm on the low-heat setting for about 30 minutes to warm through.

SERVE Ladle the soup into individual bowls and serve right away.

Cranberry Bean
and
Farro Soup

A perfect winter dish, this soup feels at once both healthy and comforting.
It calls for chewy, nutty farro, which marries well with the creamy texture
and subtle flavor of the beans. Leafy greens top the soup just before serving;
they slowly wilt as they are stirred in, creating a balanced meal in a bowl.

ingredients

1 cup (7 oz/220 g) dried cranberry beans

3 carrots, peeled, halved lengthwise and cut crosswise into chunks

1 large yellow onion, finely chopped

2 ribs celery, finely chopped

6 cloves garlic, sliced

6 cups (48 fl oz/1.5 l) low-sodium vegetable or chicken broth

2 sprigs fresh oregano

1 cup (7 oz/220 g) pearled farro

1 can (15 oz/470 g) diced tomatoes, drained

2 teaspoons balsamic vinegar

Kosher salt and freshly ground pepper

1 tablespoon olive oil

6 oz (185 g) thickly sliced pancetta, chopped

1½ cups (1½ oz/45 g) baby spinach

Freshly grated Parmesan cheese for garnish

makes 6 servings

step by step

PREP Pick over the cranberry beans, removing any misshapen beans or grit. Rinse under cold running water. Put the beans in a large bowl, add cold water to cover by at least 2 inches (5 cm), and let stand at room temperature overnight. Alternatively, for a quick soak, put the beans in a large pot, add water to cover by at least 2 inches, bring to a boil, remove from the heat, cover, and let soak for 1 hour. Drain and rinse the beans.

SLOW COOK Transfer the beans to the slow cooker. Add the carrots, onion, celery, garlic, broth, and oregano and stir well. Cover and cook on the low-heat setting for 4 hours.

Uncover and stir in the farro, tomatoes, vinegar, ½ teaspoon salt, and several grinds of pepper. Re-cover and continue to cook on the low-heat setting for 2 hours longer. The beans should be tender but not mushy, and the farro should be tender but still slightly firm.

ASSEMBLE About 5 minutes before the soup is ready, in a heavy frying pan over medium heat, warm the oil. Add the pancetta and sauté, stirring frequently, until the pancetta is crisp and golden, about 4 minutes. Using a slotted spoon, transfer to paper towels to drain. When the soup is ready, remove and discard the oregano sprigs.

SERVE Ladle the soup into shallow individual bowls. Top each serving with an equal amount of the spinach, then garnish with the Parmesan and pancetta and serve right away.

Spicy Red Bean
and
Chorizo Stew

This stew recalls the flavors of New Orleans and includes the "holy trinity" of vegetables that forms the foundation of Creole-style cooking: onion, celery, and bell pepper. When serving this stew, set out a bowl of freshly cooked rice and a big bottle of hot-pepper sauce, as they would in Louisiana.

ingredients

1 lb (500 g) dried red kidney beans

1 large yellow onion, finely chopped

3 ribs celery, finely chopped

1 green bell pepper, seeded and diced

6 cloves garlic, finely chopped

4 cups (32 fl oz/1 l) low-sodium beef or chicken broth

2 teaspoons red wine vinegar

3 bay leaves

1 lb (500 g) cured Spanish-style chorizo sausages, sliced ¼ inch (6 mm) thick

½–¾ teaspoon red pepper flakes

Kosher salt and freshly ground pepper

Hot-pepper sauce for seasoning

makes 6–8 servings

step by step

PREP Pick over the kidney beans, removing any misshapen beans or grit. Rinse under cold running water. Put the beans in a large bowl, add cold water to cover by at least 2 inches (5 cm), and let stand at room temperature overnight. Alternatively, for a quick soak, put the beans in a large pot, add water to cover by at least 2 inches, bring to a boil, remove from the heat, cover, and let soak for 1 hour. Drain and rinse the beans.

SLOW COOK Transfer the beans to the slow cooker. Stir in the onion, celery, bell pepper, garlic, broth, vinegar, bay leaves, chorizo, and pepper flakes to taste. Season lightly with salt and pepper. Cover and cook on the low-heat setting for 6–8 hours, stirring once or twice if possible. The beans should be very tender.

ASSEMBLE Remove and discard the bay leaves. Season the stew with salt, several grinds of pepper, and the hot-pepper sauce. If you like, using the back of a spoon, mash some of the beans against the inside of the cooker to thicken the stew.

SERVE Transfer the stew to a serving bowl and serve right away.

Italian Pasta
and
Bean Soup

Chock full of beans, pasta, and vegetables and topped with plenty
of Parmesan, this is one of my favorite cold-weather soups. If possible,
slice off the rind from a wedge of Parmesan and add it with the broth.
It will impart a lot of flavor. Accompany the soup with crusty Italian bread.

ingredients

1 lb (500 g) dried cannellini beans

4 slices thick-cut applewood-smoked bacon, diced

2 cans (14½ ounces/455 g each) diced tomatoes with juice

3 carrots, peeled and chopped

3 ribs celery, chopped

1 yellow onion, finely chopped

2 sprigs fresh thyme

1 small sprig fresh rosemary

6 cups (48 fl oz/1.5 l) low-sodium chicken broth

Kosher salt and freshly ground pepper

10 oz (315 g) small soup pasta such as ditalini or macaroni

Freshly grated Parmesan cheese for serving

makes 6—8 servings

step by step

PREP Pick over the cannellini beans, removing any misshapen beans or grit. Rinse under cold running water. Put the beans in a large bowl, add cold water to cover by at least 2 inches (5 cm), and let stand at room temperature overnight. Alternatively, for a quick soak, put the beans in a large pot, add water to cover by at least 2 inches, bring to a boil, remove from the heat, cover, and let soak for 1 hour. Drain and rinse the beans.

QUICK COOK Put the slow-cooker insert over medium heat, add the bacon, and fry until crisp, about 5 minutes. Pour off the fat from the insert.

SLOW COOK Transfer the insert to the slow cooker, add the drained beans, bacon, tomatoes and their juice, carrots, celery, onion, thyme, rosemary, and broth, and stir to mix well. Cover and cook on the low-heat setting for 8—10 hours. The beans should be very tender.

ASSEMBLE About 15 minutes before the soup is ready, bring a large pot three-fourths full of water to a boil. Add 2 tablespoons salt and the pasta and cook until al dente, according to package directions. Drain the pasta. Stir the pasta into the soup and season with salt and pepper.

SERVE Ladle into shallow individual bowls and top generously with Parmesan. Serve right away.

Chicken and Chorizo Paella
with
Roasted Red Peppers

Paella is traditionally made in a wide, shallow pan over a wood-burning fire, but that's not really practical for most of us. Here, I've re-envisioned the delicious classic for the slow cooker, where smoked paprika lends the flavor that is usually imparted by the fire. Be sure to use cured Spanish chorizo, which is different from fresh Mexican chorizo.

ingredients

2 lb (1 kg) bone-in chicken thighs, skinned (about 4 large thighs)

Kosher salt and freshly ground pepper

2 tablespoons olive oil

About 12 oz (375 g) cured Spanish-style chorizo sausage, casings removed, quartered lengthwise and sliced

1 yellow onion, finely chopped

3 cloves garlic, minced

2 teaspoons sweet smoked paprika

1 can (14½ oz/455 g) diced tomatoes with juice

1¼ cups (10 fl oz/310 ml) low-sodium chicken broth

½ cup (4 fl oz/125 ml) dry white wine

1 large pinch saffron threads, crumbled

1 cup (8 oz/250 g) chopped jarred roasted red peppers

2 cups (14 oz/440 g) short- or medium-grain white rice

Boiling water, if needed

1 cup (5 oz/155 g) thawed frozen English peas

1 lemon, cut into 8 wedges

makes 6 servings

step by step

PREP Season the chicken all over with salt and pepper.

QUICK COOK Put the slow-cooker insert on the stove top over medium-high heat, then add the oil and warm until hot. Add the chorizo, onion, garlic, and paprika and cook, stirring, until the onion is softened and the mixture is fragrant, 5–7 minutes. Stir in the tomatoes, broth, wine, saffron, 1 teaspoon salt, and a few grinds of pepper and bring to a boil.

SLOW COOK Transfer the insert to the slow cooker, stir in the roasted peppers, and immerse the chicken thighs in the mixture. Cover and cook on the low-heat setting for 5–6 hours. The chicken should be tender.

Uncover and, using a large spoon, skim off and discard any fat from the surface of the cooking liquid. Transfer the chicken thighs to a cutting board and remove and discard the bones and any fat or gristle. Shred or chop the chicken into large chunks. Return the chicken to the slow cooker and stir in the rice. Re-cover and cook on the high-heat setting until the rice is tender, 45–60 minutes, stirring once halfway through cooking so the rice cooks evenly. If the rice gets dry toward the end of cooking, stir in up to ¼ cup (2 fl oz/60 ml) boiling water.

ASSEMBLE Uncover, stir in the peas, re-cover, and let stand for 15–20 minutes to heat the peas through.

SERVE Spoon the paella onto a large platter and serve right away with the lemon wedges on the side for squeezing.

Braised Chickpeas
with
Wilted Arugula

This innovative recipe—part stew, part salad—is vegetarian, but it will
appeal to anyone looking for a satisfying, yet healthy, slow-cooked meal.
Serve with thick slices of hearty whole-grain bread to round out the meal.

ingredients

1 lb (500 g) dried chickpeas

1 large yellow onion, coarsely chopped

1 large carrot, peeled and coarsely chopped

1 stalk celery, finely chopped

3 bay leaves

3 cups (24 fl oz/750 ml) low-sodium
vegetable broth

1 can (15 oz/470 g) diced tomatoes, drained

Kosher salt and freshly ground pepper

¼ cup (4½ oz/140 g) minced red onion

2 cloves garlic

2 tablespoons red wine vinegar

6 tablespoons (3 fl oz/90 ml) extra-virgin
olive oil

2 cups (2 oz/60 g) baby arugula

makes 6 servings

step by step

PREP Pick over the chickpeas, removing any misshapen chickpeas or
grit. Rinse under cold running water. Put the chickpeas in a large bowl,
add cold water to cover by at least 2 inches (5 cm), and let stand at room
temperature overnight. Alternatively, for a quick soak, put the beans in
a large pot, add water to cover by at least 2 inches, bring to a boil, remove
from the heat, cover, and let soak for 1 hour. Drain and rinse the beans.

SLOW COOK Transfer the beans to the slow cooker. Add the onion,
carrot, celery, bay leaves, and broth and stir well. Cover and cook on the
low-heat setting for 6 hours.

Uncover and stir in the tomatoes, 1 teaspoon salt, and several grinds
of pepper. Re-cover and cook on the low-heat setting for 2 hours. The
chickpeas should be tender but not mushy.

ASSEMBLE In a bowl, whisk together the red onion, garlic, vinegar,
olive oil, ¼ teaspoon salt, and several grinds of pepper until well blended.
Add the arugula and toss to coat evenly.

Remove and discard the bay leaves from the chickpeas.

SERVE Transfer the chickpeas with a little of their braising liquid to a
large serving bowl. Top with the dressed arugula and serve right away.

Black Bean
and
Vegetable Soup

You can top this soup with various garnishes, depending on what you have
in the refrigerator: shredded Monterey jack or Cheddar cheese, a dollop of
tomato salsa or plain Greek yogurt, or chopped green onions would all work well.
I like to serve the soup with thick slices of buttered warm corn bread.

ingredients

1 lb (500 g) dried black beans

1 can (14½ oz/455 g) fire-roasted diced
tomatoes with juice

1 cup (7 oz/220 g) finely chopped jarred
roasted red peppers (3—4 peppers)

1 large yellow onion, finely chopped

1 large carrot, finely chopped

2 ribs celery, finely chopped

1 tablespoon ground cumin

1 tablespoon chili powder

6½ cups (52 fl oz/1.6 l) low-sodium chicken
or vegetable broth

Juice of 1 lime, plus more for serving

About ⅓ cup (½ oz/15 g) chopped fresh
cilantro

Kosher salt

makes 6—8 servings

step by step

PREP Pick over the black beans, removing any misshapen beans or
grit. Rinse under cold running water. Put the beans in a large bowl,
add cold water to cover by at least 2 inches (5 cm), and let stand at room
temperature overnight. Alternatively, for a quick soak, put the beans in
a large pot, add water to cover by at least 2 inches, bring to a boil, remove
from the heat, cover, and let soak for 1 hour. Drain and rinse the beans.

SLOW COOK In the slow cooker, combine the drained beans, tomatoes
and their juice, roasted peppers, onion, carrot, celery, cumin, and chili
powder. Stir well, then pour in the broth and stir well. Cover and cook
on the low-heat setting for 8—9 hours. The beans should be very tender.

Uncover and stir in the lime juice, cilantro, and 1 tablespoon salt, then
taste and adjust the seasoning. Re-cover and continue to cook on the
low-heat setting for 30 minutes longer to blend the flavors.

ASSEMBLE If you prefer a thicker soup, transfer 2 cups (16 fl oz/500 ml)
of the soup to a blender or food processor and process until smooth, then
stir the purée back into the soup.

SERVE Ladle into individual bowls and serve right away.

Asparagus, Leek, and Lemon Risotto

The slow cooker makes pretty quick work of this risotto, so don't stray too far once you have put it on to cook. Medium-thick asparagus spears are the best choice here; avoid pencil-thin or extra-thick stalks. Serve this ode-to-spring dish with a salad made with fresh peas and shaved ricotta salata for an elegant meal.

ingredients

4 tablespoons (2 oz/60 g) unsalted butter

2 leeks, white and pale green parts, trimmed, quartered lengthwise, and sliced

Kosher salt

1 tablespoon olive oil

2 cups (14 oz/440 g) Arborio or Carnaroli rice

½ cup (4 fl oz/125 ml) dry white wine

Grated zest and juice of 1 lemon, preferably Meyer

6 cups (48 fl oz/1.5 l) low-sodium chicken or vegetable broth, heated, plus more if needed

1 lb (500 g) asparagus, tough ends trimmed and spears cut crosswise on the diagonal into 1-inch (2.5-cm) pieces

½ cup (2 oz/60 g) freshly grated Parmesan cheese

makes 6 servings

step by step

QUICK COOK Put the slow-cooker insert on the stove top over medium heat, then add 2 tablespoons of the butter and warm until melted. Add the leeks and a big pinch of salt and cook, stirring, until softened, about 4 minutes. Transfer to a bowl.

Return the insert to medium heat, add the remaining 2 tablespoons butter and the oil, and warm until hot. Add the rice and cook, stirring, until toasted and golden, about 4 minutes. Add the wine and simmer, stirring occasionally, until completely absorbed, about 1 minute. Return the leeks to the insert.

SLOW COOK Transfer the insert to the slow cooker. Add the lemon zest and juice, the broth, and 1 teaspoon salt and stir to mix well. Cover and cook on the high-heat setting for 30 minutes.

Uncover and stir in the asparagus. Re-cover and continue to cook on the high-heat setting for 30 minutes longer. The rice should be tender but slightly al dente at the center of each grain and the mixture should be creamy.

ASSEMBLE Uncover and stir in the Parmesan, then taste and adjust the seasoning with salt. If the risotto is too thick, thin with hot broth to the desired consistency.

SERVE Spoon into shallow bowls or onto plates and serve right away.

Mushroom Farro Risotto

I am a big fan of the nutty flavor and chewy texture of farro, an ancient wheat strain that recalls brown rice or barley. If you have not tried it, this hearty risotto, packed with earthy mushrooms, is a great way to introduce it into your diet. Be sure to select farro that has not been precooked.

ingredients

1 tablespoon olive oil

1 tablespoon unsalted butter

½ large yellow onion, finely chopped

1½ cups (10½ oz/330 g) pearled farro

3 tablespoons dry sherry

1 lb (500 g) small cremini or button mushrooms, brushed clean and sliced

1 large carrot, peeled and finely chopped

3 sprigs fresh thyme

Kosher salt and freshly ground pepper

3 cups (24 fl oz/750 ml) low-sodium chicken or vegetable broth

½ cup (2 oz/60 g) freshly grated Parmesan cheese, plus more for serving (optional)

makes 6–8 servings

step by step

QUICK COOK Put the slow-cooker insert on the stove top over medium-high heat, then add the oil and butter and warm until the butter melts. Add the onion and cook, stirring, until lightly browned, about 3 minutes. Add the farro and cook, stirring, until lightly toasted, about 3 minutes. Stir in the sherry.

SLOW COOK Transfer the insert to the slow cooker, add the mushrooms, carrot, thyme, 2 teaspoons salt, the broth, and 1 cup (8 fl oz/250 ml) water. Cover and cook on the low-heat setting for about 3 hours. The liquid should be mostly absorbed and the farro should be tender.

ASSEMBLE Uncover, discard the thyme, and stir in the Parmesan. Taste and adjust the seasoning with salt and pepper. Let sit with the cover slightly askew (still on the low-heat setting) for 30 minutes to allow for some evaporation; the risotto will thicken slightly.

SERVE Spoon the risotto into shallow individual bowls and top with more Parmesan, if desired. Serve right away.

Artichoke Risotto

Making risotto the conventional way calls for standing at the stove and stirring steadily for 30 minutes or so, which often dissuades me from making it. Preparing risotto in a slow cooker means you can cook it largely unattended and still achieve delicious results. A Caesar salad would make a nice accompaniment to this meal.

ingredients

3 tablespoons unsalted butter

2 tablespoons olive oil

2 large shallots, finely chopped

8 cloves garlic, sliced

2 cups (14 oz/440 g) Arborio or Carnaroli rice

1 cup (8 fl oz/250 ml) dry white wine

6 cups (48 fl oz/1.5 l) low-sodium vegetable or chicken broth

Kosher salt and freshly ground pepper

½ lb (250 g) frozen artichoke hearts, thawed and halved lengthwise

¼ cup (1 oz/30 g) freshly grated Parmesan cheese

makes 6 servings

step by step

QUICK COOK Put the slow-cooker insert on the stove top over medium-high heat, then add 1 tablespoon of the butter and the oil and warm until hot. Add the shallots and cook, stirring, until lightly golden, about 6 minutes. Add the garlic and cook, stirring, for 1 minute. Add the rice and cook, stirring, until toasted and golden, about 3 minutes. Add the wine and simmer, stirring occasionally, until it has been almost completely absorbed, about 5 minutes.

SLOW COOK Transfer the insert to the slow cooker. Add the broth and 1 teaspoon salt and stir to mix well. Cover and cook on the high-heat setting for 30 minutes.

Uncover and add the artichokes, distributing them evenly. Re-cover and continue to cook on the high-heat setting for 30 minutes longer. The rice should be tender but slightly al dente at the center of each grain and the mixture should be creamy.

ASSEMBLE When the risotto is ready, stir in the remaining 2 tablespoons butter and several grinds of pepper. Taste and adjust the seasoning with salt.

SERVE Spoon the risotto into shallow individual bowls. Sprinkle the Parmesan over the top and serve right away.

Barley Risotto
with
Collard Greens

If you are looking for a stick-to-your ribs vegetarian main dish, look no further. This nutty barley risotto, studded with mushrooms, leeks, carrots, tomatoes, and hearty collard greens, is ideal for a cold winter meal. Feel free to substitute your favorite hearty greens, such as kale or chard, for the collards.

ingredients

5 tablespoons (2½ oz/75 g) unsalted butter

10 oz (315 g) button mushrooms, finely chopped

1 large carrot, peeled and finely chopped

1 leek, white and pale green part, thinly sliced

1 tablespoon minced garlic

3 tablespoons all-purpose flour

2 tablespoons tomato paste

½ cup (4 fl oz/125 ml) dry red wine

2¼ cups (18 fl oz/560 ml) low-sodium vegetable broth

1½ cups (9 oz/280 g) diced canned tomatoes with juice

1 tablespoon mild honey

½ teaspoon dried rosemary

Kosher salt and freshly ground pepper

1 cup (7 oz/220 g) pearled barley

2 cups (6 oz/185 g) thinly sliced stemmed collard greens

⅓ cup (1½ oz/45 g) freshly grated Parmesan cheese

makes 4—6 servings

step by step

QUICK COOK Put the slow-cooker insert on the stove top over medium heat, then add 2 tablespoons of the butter and warm until melted. Add the mushrooms, carrot, leek, and garlic and cook, stirring, until softened, about 10 minutes. Whisk in the flour and tomato paste and cook, stirring, until the flour is fully incorporated, about 1 minute. Pour in the wine and simmer until evaporated, about 2 minutes. Add the broth, tomatoes and their juice, honey, rosemary, 1 teaspoon salt, and a few grinds of pepper, and stir well. Increase the heat to medium-high and bring to a boil.

SLOW COOK Transfer the insert to the slow cooker and stir in the barley. Cover and cook on the low-heat setting for 4 hours. The barley should be tender.

Uncover and stir in the greens. Re-cover and cook on the high-heat setting for about 30 minutes. The greens should be tender.

ASSEMBLE Stir in the remaining 3 tablespoons butter and the cheese.

SERVE Transfer the risotto to a large shallow serving bowl or individual bowls and serve right away.

Vegetables

Winter Vegetable Stew

This cool-weather dish sparkles with color and flavor. To save time, cut up the squash, parsnips, and carrots the night before you plan to cook and serve the stew, and refrigerate them in an airtight container. Accompany the stew with a green salad and thick slices of buttered whole wheat bread.

ingredients

4 tablespoons (2 fl oz/60 ml) olive oil

1 large yellow onion, finely chopped

2 ribs celery, finely chopped

10 cloves garlic, smashed

2 tablespoons tomato paste

½ cup (4 fl oz/125 ml) medium-dry sherry

½ cup (4 fl oz/125 ml) low-sodium chicken or vegetable broth

1 teaspoon sherry vinegar or red wine vinegar

1 butternut squash, about 2½ lb (1.25 kg), peeled, seeded, and cut into 1-inch (2.5-cm) chunks

3 parsnips, peeled and cut into 1-inch (2.5-cm) chunks

3 large carrots, peeled and cut into 1-inch (2.5-cm) chunks

1 teaspoon dried tarragon

Kosher salt and freshly ground pepper

Grated zest and juice of 1 lemon

1 bunch watercress, tough stems removed and leaves chopped

makes 6 servings

step by step

QUICK COOK Place the slow-cooker insert on the stove top over medium-high heat, then add 2 tablespoons of the oil and warm until hot. Add the onion and celery and cook, stirring, until softened and beginning to brown, about 6 minutes. Add the garlic and tomato paste and cook, stirring, for 1 minute. Pour in the sherry, broth, and vinegar and deglaze the insert, stirring and scraping up any browned bits on the insert bottom with a wooden spoon.

SLOW COOK Transfer the insert to the slow cooker. Add the squash, parsnips, carrots, and tarragon, season with salt and pepper, and stir to mix well. Cover and cook on the low-heat setting for 4–5 hours, or until the vegetables are tender.

SERVE Stir the lemon juice into the stew to taste, then transfer the stew to a warmed serving bowl or shallow individual bowls. Drizzle with the remaining 2 tablespoons olive oil and top with the watercress and a sprinkle of lemon zest. Serve right away.

Slow-Cooker Ratatouille

In southern France, particularly along the Mediterranean coast, ratatouille is ubiquitous on summer menus. It is equally delicious hot, warm, or at room temperature, and tastes even better after a day in the refrigerator. The addition of fresh basil and briny capers just before serving heightens the flavors of the vegetables.

ingredients

1 eggplant, about 1 lb (500 g)

Kosher salt and freshly ground pepper

3 tablespoons tomato paste

3 tablespoons olive oil, plus more for serving

4 cloves garlic, finely chopped

1 teaspoon dried oregano

1 large yellow onion, halved and thinly sliced

2 red bell peppers, seeded and cut lengthwise into narrow strips

3 zucchini, halved lengthwise and cut crosswise into slices about ⅓ inch (9 mm) thick

4 plum tomatoes, quartered lengthwise and seeded

¼ cup (⅓ oz/10 g) finely chopped fresh flat-leaf parsley

3 tablespoons coarsely chopped fresh basil

⅓ cup (2½ oz/75 g) capers, rinsed

makes 4–6 servings

step by step

PREP Cut the eggplant into chunks about 1-inch (2.5-cm) thick. In a colander, toss the eggplant with 1 teaspoon salt, then let drain for about 30 minutes. Pat the eggplant dry with paper towels. In a small bowl, whisk together the tomato paste, olive oil, garlic, oregano, 1 teaspoon salt, and several grinds of pepper.

SLOW COOK Arrange about one-fourth each of the eggplant, onion, bell peppers, zucchini, and tomatoes in a layer in the bottom of the slow cooker. Spoon one-fourth of the tomato paste mixture over the top. Repeat to make 3 more layers each of the vegetables and the tomato paste mixture. Cover and cook on the low-heat setting for 5 hours, stirring a few times if possible. The vegetables should be tender.

SERVE Transfer the ratatouille to a serving dish and serve hot, warm, or at room temperature. Just before serving, stir in the parsley, sprinkle with the basil and capers, and drizzle with a little oil.

Summer Minestrone

This colorful vegetable soup is a great excuse to pull out the slow cooker
in the summer months. A dollop of pesto on top adds both freshness and flavor.
You can experiment with different vegetables throughout the season,
such as corn kernels, red bell peppers, and pattypan or crookneck squashes.

ingredients

2 cans (14 oz/440 g) cannellini beans,
drained and rinsed

2 cans (14½ oz/455 g) diced tomatoes
with juice

2 carrots, peeled and diced

1 yellow onion, finely chopped

2 ribs celery, finely chopped

2 Yukon gold potatoes, about ¾ lb (375 g)
total weight, peeled and cut into ½-inch
(12-mm) cubes

1 tablespoon fresh thyme leaves

6 cups (48 fl oz/1.5 l) low-sodium
chicken broth

Kosher salt and freshly ground pepper

½ lb (250 g) green beans, trimmed and
cut into 1-inch (2.5-cm) pieces

2 small zucchini, cut into ½-inch
(12-mm) cubes

Purchased or homemade pesto and freshly
grated Parmesan cheese for garnish

makes 8 servings

step by step

SLOW COOK In the slow cooker, combine the cannellini beans, tomatoes
and their juice, carrots, onion, celery, potatoes, thyme, broth, 2 teaspoons
salt, and several grinds of pepper. Stir to mix well. Cover and cook on the
low-heat setting for 5 hours.

Uncover, add the green beans and zucchini, and stir to mix well. Re-cover
and continue to cook on the low-heat setting for 1 hour. The vegetables
should be tender. Taste and adjust the seasoning with salt and pepper.

SERVE Ladle into shallow individual bowls and top each serving with
a dollop of pesto and a sprinkle of Parmesan. Serve right away.

Kale, Potato, and Sausage Soup

This hearty soup is loaded with sausage and vegetables and is perfect for
a winter evening. The addition of brown ale and sauerkraut lend the soup
additional layers of flavor. Serve this with warm brown bread and salted butter.

ingredients

1 tablespoon olive oil

1 lb (500 g) kielbasa (about 4 links), casings
removed and sausages crumbled

1 yellow onion, finely chopped

1 large carrot, peeled and finely chopped

1 rib celery, finely chopped

2 teaspoons minced garlic

¼ cup (2 oz/60 g) tomato paste

2 tablespoons Dijon mustard

1 bottle (12 oz/375 ml) brown ale

5 cups (40 fl oz/1.25 l) low-sodium
chicken broth

¼ cup (1½ oz/45 g) drained sauerkraut

Kosher salt and freshly ground pepper

1 lb (500 g) new potatoes, quartered

3 cups (9 oz/280 g) thinly sliced stemmed
kale, preferably lacinato kale

makes 4 servings

step by step

QUICK COOK Put the slow-cooker insert on the stove top over medium-
high heat, then add the oil and warm until hot. Add the sausages, onion,
carrot, celery, and garlic and cook, stirring, until the vegetables have
softened, about 7 minutes. Stir in the tomato paste and mustard and cook,
stirring, for 1 minute. Pour in the ale and simmer for 3 minutes. Add the
broth, sauerkraut, 1 teaspoon salt, and a few grinds of pepper, stir to mix
well, and bring to a boil.

SLOW COOK Transfer the insert to the slow cooker, add the potatoes,
and stir to mix well. Cover and cook on the low-heat setting for 4 hours.
The potatoes should be tender.

Uncover, add the kale, and stir to mix well. Re-cover and continue to cook
on the low-heat setting for 30—60 minutes, or until the kale is tender.

SERVE Ladle the soup into shallow individual bowls. Serve right away.

Cauliflower Cheddar Ale Soup

Rich, sweet, and nutty, this is a great soup for a cold winter's night. Avoid a hoppy beer, which can make the soup bitter. Make sure you purchase extra ale to pour at the table. Accompany the soup with thick slices of country-style levain bread.

ingredients

1¾ lb (1.75 kg) cauliflower florets

1 large yellow onion, chopped

2 large carrots, peeled and chopped

3 ribs celery, chopped

4 cups (32 fl oz/1 l) low-sodium chicken or vegetable broth, plus more, hot, if needed

1 bottle (12 fl oz/375 ml) brown or amber ale

2 tablespoons Worcestershire sauce

1 tablespoon Dijon mustard

2 bay leaves

Kosher salt and freshly ground pepper

10 oz (315 g) sharp white Cheddar cheese, shredded (2½ cups)

2 tablespoons cornstarch

makes 8 servings

step by step

SLOW COOK In the slow cooker, combine the cauliflower, onion, carrots, and celery and toss to combine. Add the 4 cups broth, the ale, the Worcestershire sauce, the mustard, the bay leaves, and 2 teaspoons salt and stir to combine. Cover and cook on the low-heat setting for 6 hours. The vegetables should be very tender.

Uncover the soup and let cool slightly. Meanwhile, in a bowl, toss together the cheese and cornstarch to coat the cheese evenly. Then, working in batches, transfer the soup to a blender or food processor and process until very smooth.

Return the soup to the slow cooker and add the cheese mixture by the handful, stirring until the cheese is melted and the soup is smooth. Re-cover and cook on the high-heat setting for 30—60 minutes to warm the soup through. If you prefer a thinner soup, stir in a little hot broth to achieve a good consistency, then taste and adjust the seasoning with salt and pepper.

SERVE Ladle the soup into shallow individual bowls. Serve right away.

Collard Greens Stew
with
Potatoes and Chorizo

This is a versatile stew that's easy to personalize. If you want to mix things up, swap out the collard greens for mustard greens or Russian or dinosaur kale, and andouille sausages in place of the chorizo. Set out a basket of crusty country bread for dipping.

ingredients

1 tablespoon olive oil

4 cured chorizo sausages, casings removed and sausages coarsely chopped

1 red onion, finely chopped

2 teaspoons minced garlic

¼ cup (2 oz/60 g) tomato paste

1½ cups (12 fl oz/375 ml) dry white wine

1 can (14 oz/440 g) diced tomatoes with juice

1 cup (8 fl oz/250 ml) low-sodium chicken broth

2 teaspoons honey

1 teaspoon hot or sweet smoked paprika

¼ teaspoon crumbled saffron threads

Kosher salt and freshly ground pepper

1 lb (500 g) new potatoes, quartered if large or halved if small

2 cups (6 oz/185 g) thinly sliced stemmed collard greens

3 tablespoons unsalted butter

makes 4 servings

step by step

QUICK COOK Put the slow-cooker insert on the stove top over medium-high heat, then add the oil and warm until hot. Add the sausages, onion, and garlic and cook, stirring, until the onion and garlic are softened, about 4 minutes. Stir in the tomato paste and cook, stirring, for 1 minute. Pour in the wine and simmer for 3 minutes. Add the tomatoes, broth honey, paprika, saffron, 1 teaspoon salt, and a few grinds of pepper, stir to mix well, and bring to a boil.

SLOW COOK Transfer the insert to the slow cooker, add the potatoes, and stir to mix well. Cover and cook on the low-heat setting for 5 hours. The potatoes should be tender.

Uncover, add the collard greens, and stir to mix well. Re-cover and continue to cook on the high-heat setting for 30—60 minutes, or until the greens are tender.

SERVE Stir in the butter, then ladle into shallow individual bowls. Serve right away.

Indian Cauliflower
and
Potato Curry

In northern India, this mild curry is traditionally cooked slowly in an earthenware pot, yielding tender vegetables bound together by a thick, creamy, fragrant sauce. The result can easily be duplicated in a slow cooker. Serve with steamed basmati rice.

ingredients

½ cup (4 fl oz/125 ml) canola oil

1 large yellow onion, coarsely chopped

1-inch (2.5-cm) piece fresh ginger, peeled and grated

1-inch (2.5-cm) piece cinnamon stick

2 teaspoons ground cumin

2 teaspoons ground coriander

2 teaspoons brown mustard seeds

1 teaspoon ground cardamom

1 teaspoon ground turmeric

½ teaspoon cayenne pepper

1 cup (8 oz/250 g) plain whole-milk yogurt (not Greek)

Kosher salt

1 lb (500 g) boiling potatoes, about 1½ inches (4 cm) in diameter, halved

1 head cauliflower, about 1½ lb (750 g), trimmed and cut into florets

1 cup (5 oz/155 g) frozen English peas

makes 6—8 servings

step by step

QUICK COOK Put the slow-cooker insert on the stove top over medium-high heat, then add the oil and warm until hot. Add the onion and cook, stirring, until starting to brown, about 8 minutes. Stir in the ginger, cinnamon, cumin, coriander, mustard, cardamom, turmeric, and cayenne and cook, stirring, until the spices are fragrant and evenly coat the onion, about 1 minute. Stir in 1 cup (8 fl oz/250 ml) hot water and deglaze the insert, stirring and scraping up the browned bits on the insert bottom with a wooden spoon. Stir in the yogurt and 2 teaspoons salt, reduce the heat to medium, and cook until the onion-yogurt mixture starts to simmer, about 5 minutes.

SLOW COOK Transfer the insert to the slow cooker, add the potatoes and cauliflower, and stir to mix with the onion-yogurt mixture. Cover and cook on the low-heat setting for 3—4 hours, or until the vegetables are tender and the sauce is thick.

ASSEMBLE About 30 minutes before the vegetables are ready, add the peas, stir gently, re-cover, and cook until heated through.

SERVE Remove and discard the cinnamon stick, then spoon the curry onto individual plates. Serve right away.

Eggplant Stew
with
Chickpeas and Raisins

This satisfying stew, redolent with Indian-style spices, is so delicious, no one
will guess that it is vegan. Serve it over rice or with warmed Indian bread.
Accompany with a tomato and cucumber salad and offer mango sorbet for dessert.

ingredients

2 tablespoons coconut or canola oil

1 yellow onion, finely chopped

1 green bell pepper, seeded and
finely chopped

1 small jalapeño chile, minced

2 teaspoons minced garlic

2 teaspoons peeled and minced
fresh ginger

2 tablespoons tomato paste

2 cups (16 fl oz/500 ml) low-sodium
vegetable broth

1 teaspoon curry powder

Kosher salt and freshly ground pepper

3 Asian eggplants, peeled and cut into
½-inch (12-mm) cubes (about 5 cups/
13 oz/410 g)

1 can (29 oz/910 g) chickpeas, drained
and rinsed

½ cup (3 oz/90 g) raisins

⅓ cup (½ oz/15 g) finely chopped
fresh cilantro

makes 4 servings

step by step

QUICK COOK Put the slow-cooker insert on the stove top over medium
heat, then add the oil and warm until hot. Add the onion, bell pepper, chile,
garlic, and ginger and cook, stirring, until softened, about 6 minutes. Stir
in the tomato paste and cook, stirring, for 1 minute. Add the broth, curry
powder, 2 teaspoons salt, and a few grinds of pepper, stir to mix well,
and bring to a boil.

SLOW COOK Transfer the insert to the slow cooker, add the eggplant,
chickpeas, and raisins, and stir to mix well. Cover and cook on the
high-heat setting for 2½ hours. The eggplant should be very tender.

SERVE Stir in the cilantro and transfer to a serving bowl or individual
plates. Serve right away.

Butternut Squash
and
Chickpea Curry

Even serious carnivores will find this hearty vegan curry delicious. I like to serve it spooned over steamed rice, with a dollop of tamarind chutney or some plain Greek yogurt. It is also great with warmed naan instead of rice.

ingredients

3 cans (15 oz/470 g each) chickpeas, drained and rinsed

1 butternut squash, 3—3½ lb (1.5—1.75 g), peeled, seeded, and cut into ½-inch (12-mm) cubes

1 large yellow onion, finely chopped

4 cloves garlic, minced

2 tablespoons peeled and grated fresh ginger

4 teaspoons ground coriander

2½ teaspoons ground turmeric

½ teaspoon red pepper flakes (optional)

3 cups (24 fl oz/750 ml) coconut milk

¼ cup (⅓ oz/10 g) chopped fresh cilantro, plus more for garnish (optional)

Kosher salt

Juice of 1 large lemon

Chopped green onion for garnish (optional)

makes 8 servings

step by step

SLOW COOK In the slow cooker, combine the chickpeas, squash, onion, garlic, ginger, coriander, turmeric, pepper flakes (if using), coconut milk, 1 cup (8 fl oz/250 l) water, cilantro, and 1 teaspoon salt. Stir to mix well. Cover and cook on the low-heat setting for 4 hours. The squash should be very tender.

SERVE Stir in the lemon juice and taste and adjust the seasoning with salt if needed. Ladle into shallow bowls, garnish with cilantro or green onion, and serve right away.

Creamy Vegetable
and
Leek Soup

This cool-weather soup appears humble, but once you taste it, you will discover
that it is wonderfully silky and rich. Be sure to purée it as smoothly as possible.
If you have time, for an extra-smooth result, pass the puréed soup through
a fine-mesh sieve. Serve this with an orange, shaved fennel, and bitter greens salad.

ingredients

1½ lb (750 g) Yukon gold potatoes, peeled
and cut into 1-inch (2.5-cm) chunks

1½ lb (750 g) celery root, peeled and
cut into 1-inch (2.5-cm) chunks

1 lb (500 g) parsnips, peeled and cut
into 1-inch (2.5-cm) chunks

2 leeks, white and pale green parts, halved
lengthwise and thinly sliced crosswise

6 cups (48 fl oz/1.5 l) low-sodium chicken
broth, plus more if needed

Kosher salt and freshly ground pepper

½ cup (4 fl oz/125 ml) heavy cream

makes 8 servings

step by step

SLOW COOK In the slow cooker, combine the potatoes, celery root,
parsnips, leeks, 6 cups broth, and 1 tablespoon salt and stir to mix well.
Cover and cook on the low-heat setting for 6 hours. The vegetables should
be very tender.

ASSEMBLE Uncover and let cool slightly, then, working in batches,
transfer the soup to a blender and process until very smooth. If needed,
add more broth to achieve the consistency you like. Return the soup to
the slow cooker and stir in the cream, then taste and adjust the seasoning
with salt and pepper. Re-cover and continue to cook on the low-heat
setting for about 30 minutes to warm through.

SERVE Ladle into individual bowls and serve right away.

Spiced Acorn Squash
with
Garlic-Mint-Yogurt Sauce

Because of its dense, hearty texture, winter squashes are a wonderful ingredient on which to center a vegetarian main course. This dish borrows the flavors of Afghanistan—warm spices, tomatoes, yogurt, garlic, and mint—to create a memorable dish. Serve it with a cucumber salad and whole-grain bread to complete the meal.

ingredients

2½ lb (1.25 kg) acorn squash

½ cup (2 fl oz/60 ml) canola oil

1-inch (2.5 cm) piece fresh ginger, peeled and grated

1 teaspoon ground coriander

½ teaspoon ground cinnamon

½ teaspoon red pepper flakes

1 can (14½ oz/455 g) tomato sauce

½ cup (4 oz/125 g) sugar

Kosher salt and freshly ground pepper

1 cup plain whole-milk Greek yogurt

2 cloves garlic, minced

3 tablespoons chopped fresh mint

makes 4–6 servings

step by step

PREP Using a large knife, cut the squash in half lengthwise. Scoop out the seeds with a large spoon, then cut the squash into 1½-inch (4-cm) pieces. If desired, put the squash pieces in a locking plastic bag and refrigerate up to overnight.

QUICK COOK In the slow cooker insert over medium-high heat, warm the oil. Working in batches if necessary, add the squash to the insert and sauté until evenly browned, about 7 minutes. Transfer to a plate. Add the ginger, coriander, cinnamon, and pepper flakes and sauté until fragrant, about 30 seconds. Sir in the tomato sauce, sugar, ½ teaspoon salt, and a few grinds of pepper and bring to a boil.

SLOW COOK Transfer the insert to the slow cooker. Add the browned squash to the insert and stir to combine it with the tomato sauce mixture. Cover and cook until the squash is very tender and the sauce is thick, 2 hours on the high-heat setting or 4 hours on the low-heat setting.

Meanwhile, in a bowl, stir together the yogurt, garlic, mint, and ½ teaspoon salt. Cover and refrigerate until serving time.

SERVE Transfer the squash and tomato sauce to a platter or individual plates. Serve right away, passing the yogurt mixture at the table for topping individual portions.

Spring Vegetable Ragout

This is the perfect way to use spring's bounty of vegetables, including new potatoes, leeks, and baby artichokes. Serve alongside soft polenta, or top with fried or poached eggs for a heartier meal. For a vegetarian dish, omit the bacon.

ingredients

6 oz (185 g) new potatoes or small red potatoes, cut into 1-inch (2.5-cm) pieces

3 leeks, white and pale green parts, halved lengthwise, then cut crosswise ¼ inch (6 mm) thick

1 lb (500 g) fresh baby artichokes, trimmed and halved lengthwise, or 1 package (14 oz/440 g) frozen artichoke hearts, thawed and halved lengthwise

1 cup (6 oz/185 g) cherry or grape tomatoes, halved

10 cloves garlic, smashed

½ yellow onion, finely chopped

¼ cup (2 fl oz/60 ml) dry white wine

¼ cup (2 fl oz/60 ml) low-sodium vegetable or chicken broth

2 tablespoons olive oil

4 teaspoons white wine vinegar

2 sprigs fresh thyme

Kosher salt and freshly ground pepper

4 slices bacon

1½ cups (7½ oz/235 g) fresh or thawed frozen English peas

1 tablespoon chopped fresh mint

1 tablespoon chopped fresh basil

makes 4–6 servings

step by step

SLOW COOK In the slow cooker, combine the potatoes, leeks, fresh artichokes (if using frozen hearts, reserve for adding later), tomatoes, garlic, onion, wine, broth, oil, vinegar, thyme, ½ teaspoon salt, and several grinds of pepper and stir to mix well. Cover and cook on the low-heat setting for 3 hours. If using frozen artichoke hearts, add them to the slow cooker after 2 hours of cooking and stir well. The vegetables should be tender.

ASSEMBLE In a frying pan over medium heat, fry the bacon until crisp, about 5 minutes. Transfer to paper towels to drain. About 30 minutes before the ragout is ready, add the peas, re-cover, and cook until the peas are warmed through.

SERVE Remove and discard the thyme, then stir in the mint and basil. Transfer the vegetables and some of their juices to a serving bowl or individual plates. Crumble the bacon into large pieces and scatter over the top. Serve right away.

INDEX

weldon**owen**

415 Jackson Street, 3rd Floor, San Francisco, CA 94111
www.weldonowen.com

QUICK SLOW COOKING

Conceived and produced by
Weldon Owen, Inc.
In collaboration with
Williams-Sonoma, Inc.
3250 Van Ness Avenue
San Francisco, CA 94109

A WELDON OWEN PRODUCTION

Printed and bound in China by
1010 Printing, Ltd.

First printed in 2014
10 9 8 7 6 5 4 3 2 1

Library of Congress Control
Number: 2014941596

ISBN 13: 978-1-61628-825-9
ISBN 10: 1-61628-825-6

Weldon Owen is a division of
BONNIER

WELDON OWEN, INC

CEO and President Terry Newell
VP, Sales and Marketing Amy Kaneko
VP, Publisher Roger Shaw

Associate Publisher
  Jennifer Newens
Associate Editor Emma Rudolph

Creative Director Kelly Booth
Art Director Ali Zeigler
Senior Production Designer
  Rachel Lopez Metzger

Production Director Chris Hemesath
Associate Production Director
  Michelle Duggan

Photographer Eva Kolenko
Food Stylist Lillian Kang
Prop Stylist Glenn Jenkins

ACKNOWLEDGEMENTS

Weldon Owen wishes to thank the following people for their
generous support in producing this book: Amanda Anselmino, Ashley Batz,
Rachel Boller, Dina Cheney, Brian Lackey, Eve Lynch, Amber McKee,
Elizabeth Parson, Sharon Silva, and Sharpe and Associates